100 Activities to
Help You *Relax, Recharge,*
and *Rebalance Your Life*

SELF-CARE
for
EMPATHS

TANYA CARROLL RICHARDSON

ADAMS MEDIA
New York London Toronto Sydney New Delhi

Adams Media
An Imprint of Simon & Schuster, Inc.
100 Technology Center Drive
Stoughton, MA 02072

First Adams Media hardcover edition September 2020

ADAMS MEDIA and colophon are trademarks of Simon & Schuster.

For information about special discounts for bulk purchases, please contact Simon & Schuster Special Sales at 1-866-506-1949 or business@simonandschuster.com.

The Simon & Schuster Speakers Bureau can bring authors to your live event. For more information or to book an event contact the Simon & Schuster Speakers Bureau at 1-866-248-3049 or visit our website at www.simonspeakers.com.

Interior design by Priscilla Yuen
Images © Getty Images/kate_sun

Manufactured in the United States of America

3 2021

Library of Congress Cataloging-in-Publication Data
Names: Richardson, Tanya Carroll, 1974- author.
Title: Self-care for empaths / Tanya Carroll Richardson.
Description: First Adams Media hardcover edition. | Avon, Massachusetts: Adams Media, 2020.
Includes bibliographical references and index.
Identifiers: LCCN 2020017510 | ISBN 9781507214121 (hc) | ISBN 9781507214138 (ebook)
Subjects: LCSH: Sensitivity (Personality trait) | Empathy. | Mindfulness (Psychology)
Classification: LCC BF698.35.S47 R53 2020 | DDC 158--dc23
LC record available at https://lccn.loc.gov/2020017510

ISBN 978-1-5072-1412-1
ISBN 978-1-5072-1413-8 (ebook)

ACKNOWLEDGMENTS

First and foremost, I'd like to thank the thousands of empath clients I've spoken with in intuitive sessions. The deep connection and vulnerability you brought allowed my work to truly be my passion. I've learned so much from you! Spiritual teachers/empaths like Robert Ohotto, Sonia Choquette, Tess Whitehurst, Judith Orloff, Cheryl Richardson, Radleigh Valentine, Lee Harris, Elaine Aron, Colette Baron-Reid, Tosha Silver, and so many others have been invaluable in helping me discover, nurture, and understand that precious sensitive part of myself. I've been blessed to have so many empath friends—too many to name here. So I'll simply thank one of my oldest and dearest—Amy. I'd also like to acknowledge *all* my family and friends, who have been incredibly supportive of my work, as well as my angels—I'd be lost without them. Lastly, I'd like to thank the professional writers and editors who helped me hone my craft over the years and gave me opportunities to publish. You know who you are and I'm forever grateful.

CONTENTS

4

CHAPTER 4

Nurture Your Own Energy 95

CHAPTER 5

Work with the Energy of Spaces 125

CHAPTER 6
Create Balance and Harmony 147

INTRODUCTION

When a friend tells you over coffee about her recent breakup and starts crying, do you tear up, too—maybe even *before* she does? When your son gets accepted to his dream college, does your heart chakra (an energy center in your chest) expand, making your energy body buzz and hum? If you find yourself particularly susceptible to absorbing the energy and emotions around you, you might be an empath. Empaths have hyper-perceptive nervous and energetic systems that allow them to feel the energies and emotions of others as if they were their own.

Empaths aren't *only* capable of feeling more from those in their intimate circle and immediate vicinity, like friends, family members, and coworkers, however—they can also be affected by global energy or something happening to a person, animal, or place they have only read about in the news. An empath can even sense things happening when they haven't been told anything at all!

It's a deeply connecting experience to be able to feel more of the emotions and energies in the room or even the world. But feeling so much can also be taxing. You might tire easily, find your mind filled with ongoing chatter, or feel emotionally drained.

The self-care activities in this book are specially designed to help you overcome these challenges so you can enjoy the blessing of your magical empath nature. Working as a professional intuitive, I've had the opportunity to get to know thousands of empaths from all over the globe and all walks of life. From their experiences and my own, I've cultivated one hundred empath-specific self-care tools to help you enjoy and engage with the world around you in a more nourishing, empowered way. The exercises, quizzes, and rituals in this book will help you:

- Stay grounded by identifying issues that typically frazzle, drain, and overwhelm most empaths.
- Avoid burnout by utilizing your powerful sixth sense to mindfully tune in or out of others.
- Remain centered in your own energy instead of trying to manage another person's emotional experience.
- Retreat and recover to rebalance your sensitive system and emerge refreshed and energized.
- Support your physical body to develop more energetic and emotional stamina so life feels magical, meaningful, and joyful.
- Work with the energy of spaces to create an empath sanctuary environment.

When you focus on your self-care with these ideas (and dozens more), you can better manage your sensitivity so that, depending on the situation, you can set boundaries with people and collective energy or open up to feel in to people and situations. You'll learn how to create, identify, manage, and harness energy, as well as how to practice techniques that support your sensitive nervous and energetic systems every day. This book encourages you to create healthier relationships with others, advocate for yourself, process your emotions, and make the most of your ability. With practice and mindfulness, you can learn to turn the volume up or down on your sensitivity, and regularly re-ground back in to your own energy or come home to yourself.

Feeling more—from everything and everyone—can greatly enhance your human experience. Being an empath is a magical way to travel through life, and the tools in this book will help enrich your own empath journey, making it more fun and more fulfilling. Keep your unique body, mind, and spirit balanced, healthy, and happy with *Self-Care for Empaths*!

CHAPTER 1

Understand Your Empath Nature

Think of being an empath as having a more open or porous emotional and energetic system. For example, the person sitting at work next to you might be naturally wired to be attuned to their own energies and emotions, but you as an empath are wired to pick up on your energies and emotions *and* those of others around you. So the micromanager at work may not bother your coworker but might really get under your empath skin. That's because the anxious energy of this micromanager can sometimes register in your own system (we'll address how to better protect against that throughout this book).

Or you could be invited to the wedding of someone you really don't know well and still feel incredibly touched as the couple is toasted by loved ones, dances around the room, and gazes at each other adoringly. Someone else at the wedding might marvel at how deeply this is affecting or moving you, since you barely know the couple. Your strong emotional reaction occurs because you are able to feel the couple's joy and tenderness as if it were your own. That's just part of being an empath.

In this first chapter, we'll explore your empath nature so you can better understand this fascinating, layered aspect of yourself and why you need special self-care tools to maintain harmony and balance in your life.

WHAT IT MEANS TO BE AN EMPATH

Empaths have a few key qualities in common. To determine if you might be an empath or identify which empath qualities are most prominent in you, ask yourself the following questions.

- Do I sometimes feel overflowing with emotion, like bursting with excitement when something great happens in my life or deeply sad for a friend who is going through a hard time? (Empaths not only feel a lot; they can feel things deeply and intensely.)

- Do I experience other people's energies and emotions so intimately that it's as if other people's energies and emotions are my own? (This is the hallmark trait of an empath.)

- Can I often sense what is really going on with someone emotionally, whether they share this verbally/with facial expressions or not? (When someone is trying to conceal or mask their own emotions, empaths can usually tell quickly what the real emotional story is going on underneath.)

- Am I very moved by the energy of spaces? (Empaths can feel at home and comfortable—or feel very much not at home and uncomfortable—in a certain house or park or office. Empaths also understand that spaces have collective energy that has built up over time.)

- Do people tend to want to open up and share their emotional experience with me? (Just being around an empath's energy has the ability to make others get in touch with and want to process their own emotional experiences.)

- Can I feel the energy in plants, trees, bodies of water, and crystals? (Empaths are very sensitive to energy and naturally understand that it resides in everything.)

- Do I get physical cues about energy and emotions, such as chills when someone shares something that resonates with me or brief nausea when someone near me is feeling sick? (Some empaths are so sensitive they can feel, temporarily, the physical states of other people.)

- Am I afraid I will get overwhelmed by the energies and emotions of others? (Empaths sometimes feel the need to hide out as a way to cope with emotional and energetic overwhelm.)

- Have parents or partners accused me of being too sensitive or too emotional? (If so, know that you don't need to feel shame for being sensitive to energy or feeling emotions deeply—whether you're an empath or not.)

- Am I incredibly moved by the stories of animals and people I read about in books, hear about in the news, or see in the movies? (Empaths have an energetic heart that is easily touched by others, even fictional characters or people and animals they have never met.)

- Is it sometimes difficult for me to be assertive and get my needs met if standing up for what I want will cause uncomfortable emotions in someone else? (Since empaths easily absorb other people's energies and emotions, they can fall into people-pleasing tendencies.)

- Do I sometimes feel as if I lose myself in romantic relationships, or have a little piece of my heart taken away when someone leaves my life? (Empaths can bond intensely and quickly with people and sometimes struggle with codependency.)

- Do I cry easily, like when I am moved by something I see on television or when someone else I know is upset or happy? (Empaths are easily moved by things outside of themselves, which can bring on the waterworks.)

- Does life seem full of wonder to me, and do I get great meaning out of small moments that others might miss or feel are insignificant? (Because empaths pick up easily on subtle stimuli, they can live passionately and feel big feels from "small" experiences.)

If you answered yes to many of these questions, you are probably an empath. Keep in mind each empath will be somewhat unique in the way they experience this phenomenon, and that you might amass more experiences over time. You could initially answer no to some of these questions but then say yes several years later. Whether you have been having these empath experiences since you were a young child or the empath in you has only more recently awakened, you'll find support in this book.

FINDING YOUR PLACE IN THE WORLD

Being an empath is simply the way you were set up to experience life: by feeling and sensing more. It's not necessarily good or bad, right or wrong—just a little different!

Your power comes by realizing that your empathic ability is simply part of how your internal GPS is naturally wired to navigate life.

Empaths are often subject to generalizations and myths that falsely define them. For example, your sensitivity does not make you weak or too emotional, nor does it hold you back from experiencing the larger world—empaths can have any type of profession, for example. On the other hand, being an empath doesn't mean that you are inherently wiser, more enlightened, more gifted, or more worthy than anyone else.

While empaths may need to be more mindful of the amounts and types of energies and emotions they expose themselves to, being an empath is not an excuse to opt out of the more challenging emotional and energetic situations in life. Life is full of ups and downs, and if you opt out of the tougher parts to protect your sensitive system, you will unfortunately also miss out on the rewarding experiences too.

If you ever feel you just can't handle life, please don't judge yourself. That's a sign you need more support. Getting more support when you need it is a crucial part of healthy self-care. We all need help getting through this life, whether we are an empath or not! You might turn to the assistance of loved ones, trusted colleagues, and/or healthcare professionals in addition to the exercises in this book. Be sure to practice radical self-love too (we'll work on that in an exercise later on).

THE FOUR MAIN PSYCHIC PATHWAYS

To better understand yourself as an empath, it helps to learn how the four main psychic pathways—*clairaudience*, or hearing intuitive guidance; *claircognizance*, or knowing intuitive guidance; *clairvoyance*, or seeing intuitive guidance; and *clairsentience*, or feeling intuitive guidance— operate in your everyday life. When you understand your own system, you'll know how to better nurture it, and part of an empath's system is a strong intuition, or sixth sense. Your intuition, which gives you guidance via the four main psychic pathways, helps you navigate the world—and it can also help you navigate yourself. Among other things, your intuition will give you guidance about how to better take care of yourself, or alert you to self-care issues that need your attention. While I use all four "clairs" in sessions with clients, I also rely on them in my personal life for compassionate, comprehensive self-care.

These terms—the four "clairs"—might seem fancy, but they can be explained in simple language. For example, all empaths are naturally strong in the clairsentience, or feeling, psychic pathway. *Clairsentience* is that feeling you get when a major purchase, like a home, is a good one or meant for you—perhaps you sense warm, inviting, positive energy around this home, or feel unexplainably at home when you walk through the door for the first time with a real estate agent. Or it could be the uncomfortable, something-is-off vibe you get while interviewing at a new company. This type of energetic or emotional impression is naturally quite developed for most empaths. While it may not be something we can see with the naked eye, for empaths, energy and vibes are things we can feel very clearly, and should never discount.

Empaths can easily access this clairsentient psychic pathway. But you might be less familiar with the other three psychic pathways. Like with any other skill set, the more you practice and use these pathways, the more adept you may become at them. Keep in mind that clairaudience and clairvoyance are the rarer psychic pathways to have open, yet you don't need to be able to access those to have rockstar intuition.

- **Clairaudience:** Hearing intuitive guidance as a voice in your head that is not your own. The voice will sound calm and offer helpful advice. (This voice is different than the voices people with mental illnesses or severe vitamin and mineral deficiencies or hormone imbalances can experience, which might be distracting or unpleasant.)

- **Clairvoyance:** Seeing intuitive guidance as images in your mind. Sometimes these images will be straightforward, like seeing the image of a friend's face when you're wondering whom to confide in. But the images can also appear as a metaphor, like seeing a lush landscape of dark, fertile soil and lots of vibrant green plant life when you're pondering the future possibilities of a romantic or business relationship.

- **Claircognizance:** Knowing intuitive guidance, often as aha moments or mental downloads that appear in your mind fully formed. These are thoughts that pop into your head and are often out-of-the-box solutions, not thoughts that are emotionally charged or conclusions you got to by logical deduction.

While some of the concepts in this workbook are very mystical, they'll become less intimidating when you approach them in a practical way. That's really important for a grounded empath to remember.

Explore the Four Main Psychic Pathways

Pick one of the psychic pathways and concentrate on using it more mindfully for one week. Your intuitive system is unique, just like you, so you might find you're naturally stronger in one or two psychic pathways—but feel free to play with them all, knowing that a new-for-you psychic pathway *could* open up anytime! This exercise will help you understand and develop your intuition so you can better recognize all the important self-care guidance it sends.

- **Clairvoyance:** Pay attention to the images that pop into your mind but are not obviously attached to a thought, like thinking of your mom and seeing her face. To kick-start clairvoyance, meditate once a day for 10 minutes, and see what images come as your eyes are closed—or open. This is all about receiving. Let the images arrive without forcing them.

- **Claircognizance:** Observe the thoughts that appear in your mind fully formed, out of the blue, as out-of-the-box solutions to problems or different angles on situations, like thinking your boss's blistering critique of your performance is more about her own stress levels due to her challenging situation at home than it is about you. Look for fresh insight.

- **Clairaudience:** Notice if you hear a calm, comforting voice in your mind that is not a thought and not your own voice. You might hear one word or full sentences. Clairaudience is probably the rarest psychic pathway to have open. For me it opened around the age of thirty and took some getting used to! If you don't hear a voice in your mind, pay attention to the words you hear others speak, whether it's overhearing something poignant at the grocery store or hearing a line in a movie that speaks to a challenge you're facing. This is also intuitive guidance.

- **Clairsentience:** This psychic pathway is your empath superpower! Focus on the emotional, energetic, and even physical sensations that could be coming from your intuition. Help activate or enhance clairsentience by connecting with your heart chakra. Each day, for a few minutes, find a quiet place to sit with your hand over your heart. Notice any sensations you feel.

Intuition is not a substitute for consulting your logical brain, experts, or past experiences in the world—but your sixth sense is an important complement to those things. So use it!

SPECIAL SELF-CARE NEEDS OF EMPATHS

Being an empath makes you a little different, which means your self-care practices need to be a little different too. Because you have hyper-perceptive nervous and energetic systems that pick up more easily on subtle stimuli, you are more prone to overstimulation and will need to build mindful retreat-and-recover time into your schedule.

Retreat-and-recover time involves unplugging your nervous and energetic systems from the larger grid and doing things that are more low stimulation, where there is simply less of others' energies and emotions to take in. Classic examples of retreat-and-recover time are reading quietly beside a partner before bed or getting lost in a solo creative project, like knitting on a lazy Saturday afternoon. Retreat-and-recover time is just one of the many empath-specific self-care practices we'll cover in this book, but it's an important one.

Because energy is something you're very sensitive to, learning how to nurture, connect with, and manage your own energy is another important self-care tool. Processing your emotions, and developing empath-friendly techniques to do so, helps you avoid getting caught up in the emotions of others. Just because you can feel other people's emotions does not mean you are *responsible* for their emotions. Paying more attention to your own emotional experience helps you avoid going into that of others in an unhealthy way.

While empaths are naturally wired to tune in to the energies and emotions around them, you can learn to mindfully tune in—or tune out—by engaging witnessing energy. We'll look at different situations and why you might choose to tune in or out in each. Balance is the golden rule for empaths, and we'll cover ways to cultivate more balance in all areas of your life, including creating more energetic balance in your physical home.

If you already have some self-care activities that you practice, you can continue doing those as well. For example, eating a healthy diet, taking supplements or medication, getting plenty of rest, exercising in moderation, having nourishing relationships, finding emotional support, being of service or giving back, engaging in activities that light you up, and maintaining a good work-life balance are self-care principles that work for anyone.

THE IMPORTANCE OF STAYING GROUNDED

"Grounded empath" is a phrase you'll see throughout the book. But when people talk about being "grounded," what do they really mean? They might be referring to taking care of practical things, like filing your taxes on time or remembering to take supplements and medication every day. Or they could be referring to a feeling of being secure—feeling calm, confident, safe, and open. Or they could mean grounding yourself by standing with your feet on the earth, connecting you to its energy and power. All of those definitions of being grounded work for the topic of self-care.

For empaths, being grounded is feeling centered in yourself and your own emotional and energetic systems. Staying grounded is essential for empaths because empaths experience more invitations or excuses to go in to the energy of others because they can so easily pick up on the energy of others. That's why we'll talk about it so much in this book, and why there's a chapter dedicated to keeping yourself grounded (see Chapter 2). Being an empath is truly a magical, mystical path. But what gives you the most access to your empath sensitivity—and an ability to better manage, guide, maximize, and even control that sensitivity—is being very grounded in an earthy, practical way.

Maintaining a mindful self-care practice is the best way to stay grounded. That includes the practical aspects of staying grounded—keeping your life running in a smooth, orderly, pleasant manner—which is why we even touch on financial health in this book.

There will be times in your life when, because of certain circumstances (like a health, relationship, or financial challenge), you struggle to feel grounded. Those are the times to lean in even more to a routine of mindful self-care. Taking care of yourself will help you feel like your life has some sort of predictable rhythm you can trust. This book is here to help you find that rhythm.

Create a Nature Heart Mandala

Rituals are a mindful way for empaths to reconnect to their own energy! Rituals require presence and focus, and can help you ground yourself. In this ritual, you'll get clearer on the larger meaning, for you personally, of being an empath. How does being an empath serve you, and how might it also serve others—like in your relationships, activism, or profession?

In Sanskrit, *mandala* means "circle," referring to symbolic art used in Buddhist and Hindu religions for sacred ceremonies, practices, and meditations. Mandalas represent the universe and how everything is connected—as an empath you can feel intimately connected to the larger world. Many empaths feel more centered and calm in nature, and working with nature elements can have a similar effect.

For this exercise, you'll need beautiful, interesting nature elements procured in a sustainable way, such as fresh flowers from a farmers' market, leaves fallen from a tree in your backyard or neighborhood park, or rocks purchased at a local garden center. Collect an assortment of objects of different sizes, shapes, and colors, like shells, twigs, pine cones, and feathers, then follow these steps.

1. Locate a place in your home where the mandala can sit undisturbed. Avoid high-traffic areas and places pets frequent. If you have small children, explain that this is a special piece of art close to your heart that everyone can enjoy looking at but not touching.

2. Mandalas are a sacred endeavor, so decide how you can make the experience feel more sacred. For example, you could listen to sacred music during the construction or say a quick prayer or blessing before you begin.

3. Have fun arranging your objects in the shape of a heart, symbolic of your energetic empath heart. (Search for images of nature mandalas online for inspiration if you like.) Get creative. Become lost in the process.

4. Notice your state of mind as you construct this mandala. Does your mind quiet and enter a meditative state? Do memories, emotions, and interesting thoughts bubble up? Rituals can be an awakening, healing experience. Keep coming back to gentle questions, like "Why am I an empath?" and "How does this/can this serve me and possibly others?"

5. Say another blessing as you close the ritual. Stand back and take in your mandala. Put your hand over your heart chakra and take a few deep breaths to ground yourself.

6. If you feel comfortable, share an image of your mandala on social media with the hashtag #groundedempath or #empathselfcare. Or you might feel more comfortable sharing this creation with only a few trusted loved ones.

7. Keep your mandala out on display for at least a few days. Add things if you feel inspired. When the insights you wanted have arrived, or the energy of your mandala feels less alive or inspiring and more neutral or even stagnant, lovingly disassemble it. Consider composting the nature elements. Take a moment to thank them for their gifts!

CHAPTER 2

Stay Grounded

Feeling your own energies and emotions as well as those of others as if they were your own is a deep emotional experience that most empaths cherish. Yet being an empath also has its challenging aspects: Because you are sensing more, you can more easily become overstimulated, which can lead to more easily feeling frazzled, overwhelmed, or drained. You might have to be more mindful of staying connected to yourself and prioritizing your own energies and emotions since you can so immediately and intimately tune in to others. Your self-care practice, which will include empath-specific self-care techniques, is your best shield against empath burnout.

In this chapter, we'll explore how to avoid (or at least minimize) some of the more distracting or destabilizing aspects of being an empath so you can savor all the good stuff. And there is so much good stuff! When an empath is feeling grounded—stable, calm, confident, and centered in their own energies and emotions—life can truly be a magical, miraculous journey.

Identify Your Top Empath Energy Drains

As an energy-sensitive person, you have to protect your own energy against situations that drain you. I've listed eighteen common empath energy drains. And here are three ways to use this list to identify what could currently be draining in your life.

OPTION 1: Use your intuition.
Instead of reading through the following items, use your intuition to arrive at a number between one and eighteen. Feel in to each number, see a number in your mind, hear a number in your mind, or experience a deep knowing about a number as a thought. That number (or numbers) corresponds to your top drain.

OPTION 2: Focus on the present.
Read through the following list and, after reading each entry, determine the top, or top three or four, empath energy drains active in your life right now.

OPTION 3: Reflect on your past.
Read through the following list and identify the top drains you've struggled with in the past. The following situations can be particularly draining for empaths:

- Procrastinating or letting important tasks pile up.
- Overcommitting yourself.
- Overexposing yourself to violence on television, in the movies, or in the news.
- Trying to change someone's opinion of you by actively winning them over.
- Attempting to contain, change, or otherwise control someone else's emotional experience so you don't have to feel their challenging emotions secondhand.

- Gossiping about others or getting emotionally and mentally caught up in their lives to avoid facing your own issues.
- Worrying about what other people think of you.
- Avoiding potentially emotional confrontations that might be healthy or serve you because you fear absorbing someone else's emotional reaction.
- Not getting enough personal space in an intimate relationship.
- Trying to talk yourself out of an emotion because the emotion might be challenging, inconvenient, or even devastating.
- Keeping the emotional peace at home or in the office at all costs.
- Being continually cast as the emotional buffer between people at home or at work.
- Being micromanaged.
- Finding yourself in tight physical quarters where you don't have much space between you and other people's bodies, or being alone in a physical space that is brand-new or very large.
- Not feeling physically comfortable: in your chair, in your clothes, and the like.
- Disliking the aesthetics of your surroundings.
- Having to be "on" around groups of people for extended periods, like at conferences or large family gatherings.
- Having someone you love or interact with daily not respect your energetic and emotional boundaries.

Once you identify your top energy drains, look for ways to minimize them. For example, if a coworker is always putting you in the middle of his conflict with his manager, offer your coworker some advice on handling this manager and then encourage his healthy personal growth by suggesting he navigate this situation on his own. You could also find a way to get support for this drain, like talking to a therapist or reading books by psychology experts.

Create Your Recipe for a Delicious Energy Day

Empaths should be especially mindful of the habits, activities, people, and places that make them feel uplifted, grounded, and peaceful. Think of these positive elements like ingredients in a recipe for a delicious energy day. Whip up one of these delicious energy days—or part of one—on a regular basis. The following prompts will help you better identify which ingredients create delicious energy in you.

- What people do you love hearing from and being around?

- Where does your energy body breathe a sigh of relief and you're so happy or relaxed that you lose track of time? (Examples: your favorite store or market, a special yoga studio, your back porch, a friend's kitchen, or a place of spiritual worship.)

- What activities help you decompress or what activities do you miss when you don't engage in them? (Examples: writing; walking; baking; knitting; reading; having a heart-to-heart chat with a close friend; hiking in nature; blowing off steam with a group of friends; dancing; playing an instrument; attending a live concert; receiving a healing service, like a massage; talking to a coach or intuitive; or cuddling with your partner or a pet before bed.)

- Which grounding routines help you feel centered and able to focus on and harness your energy? (Examples: meditating, doing a nighttime skincare routine, praying, engaging in full- or new-moon rituals, journaling, spring cleaning, practicing gratitude, or getting out of the office at lunch to take a walk.)

Make your answers to these prompts your go-tos whenever your energy feels off, but don't wait until then. Add the ingredients of delicious energy to your life every day!

Pull an Oracle Card Each Morning

Oracle decks are a divination tool that can enhance intuition (similar to tarot cards) and come with all types of themes—everything from mermaids to self-love. Selecting, or "pulling," an oracle card each morning allows you to focus your energy on something inspirational throughout the day.

When your energy is focused, you are less likely to be distracted by other people's energies and emotions. For this exercise, use a deck whose energy is soft and encouraging, like Tosha Silver's *The Wild Offering Oracle*.

1. Hold the entire deck between your palms for a few moments. Clear your mind and take a few deep breaths. Silently set the intention to pull a card that will resonate in a supportive way for you today.

2. Find your shuffling technique by experimenting with different options:

   • Gently begin mixing up the cards. When you sense it's a good time to stop, pick the card on the top or the bottom.

   • Mix up the cards, then fan them out. When a certain card grabs your attention, pick that card.

   • Mix up the cards, keeping your hold on the cards loose enough and shuffling quickly enough that a card will eventually stick out 1 to 2 inches above the others. Pick that card. A card might even fly or jump out dramatically, which is called a *jumper card.*

3. Read the words and look at the images on the card. Ask yourself how this card relates to your life specifically right now. Don't forget to consult your intuition!

4. Put the cards away and go about your day.

If you find yourself absorbed in someone else's energies and emotions, revisit the words and imagery on your card—and your curiosity about its meaning for you—as a way to ground yourself in your own energy.

> Where your thoughts go, your energy flows. When you're frazzled, drained, or overwhelmed, try to focus on something calming, healing, or inspirational to re-center yourself.

Develop a Personalized Method to Process Your Emotions

Because empaths have so much emotional information coming in (from themselves and others), it can become more challenging, at times, for an empath to identify their *own* emotions. Emotions have important messages behind them, so it's important to recognize and process your own.

The following are several techniques, especially useful to empaths, for processing emotions. You might find different techniques more useful at certain times or for certain situations. If you ever feel out of control with an emotion, seek out the help of loved ones and professionals. You deserve all the support you need.

- **Listening to music:** Is there an artist who makes you feel all the feels? Put their music on while you clean the house or make dinner. This music will be an emotional catalyst, helping you unearth what you're feeling lately. Already know you're really happy or really angry? Put on music to dance around to, or listen to music that expresses a sense of injustice—if enhancing the feeling proves too intense, transition to chill music that calms your sensitive system.

- **Moving:** Take a walk, hit the gym, or attend your favorite yoga class. If you're recovering from an injury or illness, honor the pace your body needs now. If you're restricted in your physical movement, move what you can: your hands while working on a creative project (like crafting), or any part of your body through gentle stretching. As you move, ask your body about your recent emotional experiences. The body can store emotions until you're ready to process them. Allow your mind to enter the meditative state that repetitive physical activity naturally encourages.

- **Sharing:** Connect with a trusted friend, loved one, or counselor. Let them know you'd like to talk through recent experiences to process your emotions and mindfully create space for yourself. Mention that all you require is a compassionate person who knows you well to listen. As you talk through your experiences and express feelings, notice how new insights emerge. Sharing can be an emotional release and energetic relief.

- **Journaling:** Create some empath-friendly ambiance—gentle sounds (like nature sounds), soft lighting, a clean and calm place—to write. Journal about the bigger events and emotions you've been experiencing. Resist the urge to write about what other people are doing, thinking, or feeling. Get at the messages underneath your emotions, messages like "I've been working too hard lately" or "I like this person more than I realized," by simply feeling your emotions. You might laugh or cry. An empath's life is always enhanced when they're feeling deeply and in a balanced way.

- **Connecting:** Your ability to feel the emotions of others can be a path leading back to yourself. Identify a person, either someone you know or someone in the news, going through a similar situation to your own, such as someone else also rebuilding after a financial loss, or someone else also balancing children and a career. This could even be a fictional character from a novel. As you observe this individual in circumstances similar to your own or experiencing emotions similar to yours, tap in to yourself even further.

Emotions want to be felt—and share information. Try not to label them as right or wrong. When processed, emotions can inspire you to make healthy changes in your life. Taking time to connect with yourself is key for emotional health.

Identify Unnecessary Drama

Not all drama is the same. Unnecessary drama is draining and offers little reward. Necessary drama might be draining, but the rewards can be huge—like a practical change to your circumstances or simply being true to yourself. Determining which type of drama you're facing can help you understand how to best approach it with your own self-care in mind.

Choose a frustrating situation in your life that is causing drama. Then ask yourself:

- Will this battle cost me more in the long run if I don't have it now?

- Am I backing down or backing away from drama simply because I don't want to feel the uncomfortable emotions it might create in me or someone else?

- Does this issue directly affect my well-being or the well-being of someone I love?

- Is this drama distracting me from issues that are more pressing or important?

- Will walking away or ignoring things create even more drama for me?

- Is this drama attractive or exciting to me because I'm either bored or avoiding something else I'm afraid to face?

- Is the person in the middle of this drama someone I know to be a drama king or queen, or someone who has a high tolerance for dramatic situations?

- Am I trying to protect or manage someone else's emotions by being involved, especially if this situation doesn't have much to do with me personally?

- Do I have options about how to handle this situation? If so, is it time to try a new tactic that might be effective yet involve less drama for me?

- Would there be a better time for me to engage in this drama that is both safe and beneficial to me?

Energy is a resource, and energy-sensitive empaths realize that better than anyone! After an empath's emotional, psychic, or physical energy is expended, it needs time to replenish itself—just like any other natural resource. Practice healthy conservation of your resources by managing the drama in your life.

Cocoon to Nurture Your Sensitive System

As an empath, you need to take periodic breaks from absorbing all the energies and emotions of others that you can pick up on so easily. One way to do that is by cocooning—the process of retreating and recovering in comfortable and low-stimulation environments.

Cocooning gives your sensitive system a chance to catch up with itself and ground. Cocooning can be especially useful after big events (weddings, work conferences) or emotionally triggering interactions (confrontations) where a lot of energy and emotion is flying around. You can also try preparatory cocooning before potentially emotionally stressful events, like the first week back to school. Here's how to practice cocooning.

1. Identify how much time you'll cocoon. (You can always adjust once you start, but make a plan ahead of time. For example, you might plan to cocoon for an hour and then after an hour decide to cocoon for an entire morning—or vice versa.)

2. Identify the place you'll cocoon—your apartment, a retreat center, your friend's beach house, a quiet coffee shop, or anywhere else appropriate.

3. Identify whom and/or what you'll avoid, such as avoiding checking work email or avoiding worrying about world events. (You can cocoon while still working, by the way—if needed, you could cocoon while working from home to escape the office.)

4. Identify what you'll emphasize: quiet time, creative projects, no-drama zones, or anything else gentle and nurturing.

5. Check in with yourself during the process. Do you feel isolated and need to wrap this session up sooner than you planned? Or do you

need to extend this session, or schedule another one in the future? Remember to connect with yourself for the answers!

6. After you finish, notice any differences in your system.

Whether you cocoon for an hour, an evening, a Saturday, or even longer, the low levels of stimulation will help heal your frazzled, drained, or overwhelmed system so you feel ready and eager to engage more actively with the larger world again.

Create Healthy Energetic Distance from a Certain Person or Situation

While in the previous exercise you were practicing cocooning in general, you can also go about your normal routine/day and just cocoon from one isolated issue by creating healthy energetic distance. Pulling back from one person or situation for a bit—like taking a small break from trying to solve a stressful financial situation that is safe to step back from temporarily—allows you retreat-and-recover space in a specific area of your life. It's a temporary measure while you process your emotions so you can come back into balance regarding a single issue. From that place of balance, you'll have more perspective and clarity on the situation.

1. Identify the person(s) or situation you want to create healthy energetic distance from. It might be a close, well-meaning friend who is unexpectedly being pursued by your crush (and realizing she has genuine although inconvenient feelings for your crush). Remember: You don't have to tell people you're creating healthy energetic distance from them, especially if telling them will cause unnecessary drama or hurt feelings.

2. Decide how you'll create healthy distance. In the previous example, you might keep your interactions with your close friend brief for a few days or avoid your crush's social media posts.

3. Use this healthy energetic distance time mindfully to process your emotions and think through next steps. Or use this space to move away from the situation entirely for a fresh perspective, like taking a week off from brainstorming and researching where to move. Taking a safe, healthy break from a stressful, emotional issue allows your intuition space to offer guidance.

Build In Transition Time

Transition time allows you to tune out of the last task or group of people that occupied your energy and tune back in to yourself before moving to the next task or group of people! Empaths often need mindful time to transition among roles, like parent, friend, coworker, caregiver, artist, spouse, or any other metaphorical hat they wear during the day. Empaths are so sensitive that they may embody roles easily and completely.

Use the following suggestions as inspiration to build more transition time into your daily schedule, even if it's just 5 minutes.

- Arrive 15 minutes early to an appointment or event so you can spend a few quiet moments with yourself.

- Take mindful breaks between tasks or clients at work.

- Walk around the neighborhood or sit on the porch for 20 minutes when you finish work.

- Meditate for 10 minutes after saying hello to pets, partners, roommates, or children when you walk in the door from work.

- Wake up slowly by spending 5 minutes stretching, or snuggling with a pet or partner, before getting out of bed.

- Sit down for 5 minutes and check in with your body and emotions after putting children down for a nap.

- Develop a calming evening self-care ritual before bed, like enjoying a cup of chamomile tea. Stay present and practice quieting your mind as you prepare the tea.

These types of mindful transitions allow you a moment to ground back in to your energy, instead of being thrown off-center by nonstop interactions or becoming lost in a role.

Tune In to Your Energy During Decision-Making

Empaths might struggle to get clear on what they want if they are picking up on the expectations and desires of others. For better self-care when making a decision, try the following exercise to help you tune in to yourself regarding saying yes, no, or even maybe to something.

1. Analyze the obvious pros and cons. (Example: You're an entrepreneur offered a new project. The main pro—the client is a prestigious company, so the project will raise your profile in the marketplace. The main con—turnaround time is incredibly tight, which could be stressful.)

2. Check in with your body. An empath's physical body is sensitive and will often provide intuitive information (Example: Imagine saying yes. Does your body give you green-light sensations, like feeling light or energized, or do you instead feel heaviness and exhaustion? Imagine saying no. Do you feel the relief of your shoulders relaxing, or does your tummy feel anxious at a missed opportunity?)

3. Discern what your intuition tells you about the deeper why behind this decision. Pay attention to any feelings, pictures, words, or thoughts you experience. (Example: You might get an image of yourself climbing a mountain, tired but smiling, and at the top, people you've touched with this project thank you. You have the thought "I was born for this." *Or* you might have images of mountains of paperwork piling up. Suddenly, you feel panicked. A gentle voice in your mind whispers, "Not now.")

Getting in the habit of consulting your mind, intuition, and body allows decision-making to become a more authentic, empowering process for empaths like you.

Try a Laughing Meditation

Some empaths may occasionally struggle with traditional meditation—sitting still in a quiet place for longer periods of time trying to quiet the mind and reduce thoughts. That's because empaths have more to process at the end of the day, having picked up on more by being hyper-perceptive energy-sensitives.

Laughter is healing. According to research, laughter has an anti-inflammatory effect on the body and decreases stress hormones. For empaths, laughter can also jolt their systems into ceasing the attempt to process everything they have been sensing all day. Laughter has an amazing ability to ground you in the present moment! Try the following meditation when you've had a busy day with a lot of other people's energies and emotions coming at you and you're having trouble letting it all go.

1. Watch or listen to something you know will make you laugh. Look for a light sitcom, funny movie, or stand-up special by your favorite comedian.

2. Immerse yourself in this television show, movie, or stand-up routine for 20 minutes.

3. Embrace any physical sensations that arrive, like shaking from the giggles, laughing out loud, or wiping tears from your eyes.

4. When you're done, notice if your mind is now quieter because you experienced fewer thoughts during this laughing meditation. You probably also feel more relaxed.

Part of why comedy is so popular is because it gives us a light-hearted break from our busy minds—use it intentionally to take care of yourself!

Clean Up Your Diet

You already know that a healthy diet can do wonders for your physical body, but it can also improve your sensitive system and your psychic ability. (Every empath is unique and may have special dietary requirements, so consider working with a nutritionist or health coach to help create your ideal diet.) Eating healthfully and regularly helps stabilize blood sugar and energy levels, which can give you more physical stamina for being out in the world as an empath.

Psychically, you may find your sensitivity improved on a simple, clean diet. You could experience more regular, clear intuitive hits, or a dormant psychic pathway may open up. The following suggestions can help you incorporate empath-friendly dietary practices into your routine slowly so your body can adjust and you can determine which ones work best for you.

- Drink clean, filtered water.
- Eat small meals regularly throughout the day.
- Get enough protein.
- Eat organic foods if possible.
- Watch your sugar intake.
- Emphasize low-glycemic carbs, like brown rice, and low-glycemic fruit, like berries.
- Watch your caffeine and alcohol intake.
- Take your time and chew your food.
- Eat your veggies!
- Listen to your body and how it feels and responds to different foods. Avoid foods and drinks that don't agree with you, or try an elimination diet to determine if you feel better avoiding certain foods.

Another note: Eat to feel healthy, not to look a certain way. Empaths can fall into people-pleasing, so remember that if someone is critical of your natural body type or shape, that's their problem!

If you struggle with body image issues or an eating disorder, you are not alone. Empaths might, subconsciously, feel that extra weight gives them a shield or buffer against the harsher energies and emotions in the world, or they might pick up on what culture or their family considers the ideal body type and try to match that in an effort to people-please. Body image issues and eating disorders are complex, real concerns, yet there are many tools and resources to help. Decades ago, I struggled with bulimia in high school—however, these issues can present or continue at any age. Whatever your relationship to food and body image, I'm sending you my love and support.

Sometimes the most basic self-care techniques, like eating a clean and healthy diet, can have the most profound effects. Subtle shifts and changes are often felt in a big way by sensitive empaths.

Go from Frazzled Empath to Grounded Empath

Being frazzled is the opposite of being centered. When frazzled, you may feel your energy is pulled in many different directions. This is a common issue for empaths because they can sense and then be drawn in to so many different types of energy.

Anytime you're feeling frazzled, refer to the following list of issues that can typically create a frazzled or hectic, scattered, and emotionally reactive state in empaths. Get clarity on the reasons why you're frazzled, then consider the following solutions as ways to ground yourself. If none of these issues seem like the culprit, sit down with your journal and do a loving self-inventory.

Before you read through each Frazzled Empath Trigger, ask your intuition to give you a number between one and thirteen in words, pictures, thoughts, or feelings. This might represent your top trigger now.

Frazzled Empath Trigger	Grounded Empath Solution
1 Not having enough free or unscheduled time.	Take some things off your plate and open up your schedule.
2 Existing in a chaotic living or work space.	Keep spaces clean, tidy, and uncluttered.
3 Overworking.	Set sensible office hours with clear, defined boundaries so you can come home to yourself daily.
4 Bottling up your emotions.	Find methods to express and process your own emotions with yourself and others.

Frazzled Empath Trigger	Grounded Empath Solution
5 Experiencing extreme financial pressure.	Keep unnecessary debt low to avoid its energy drain of worry and fight-or-flight-or-freeze financial fears.
6 Ignoring physical health.	Prioritize physical health with healthy food, medicine and supplements as needed, rest, gentle exercise, and staying on top of chronic health concerns.
7 Ignoring mental health issues, like anxiety and depression.	Reach out to loved ones and professionals to get help when you need it.
8 Overindulging in stimulants and depressants, like caffeine, sugar, and alcohol.	Find your own personal limits and honor them, knowing that empaths can be more sensitive to the effects of these substances.
9 Supporting a loved one—a small child, elderly parent, or struggling friend—without any breaks.	Take time to retreat and recover and ground back in to your own system regularly.
10 Chronically downplaying, hiding, or masking your own emotional experience to protect someone else's emotions.	Get honest with yourself and others about your own emotional experience in ways that feel safe and healthy.

Frazzled Empath Trigger	Grounded Empath Solution
11 Not admitting when your emotional system is over-whelmed and your nervous system is overstimulated.	Course-correct when you need to nurture yourself and regain balance.
12 Being exposed to lots of chemicals and additives in your air, food, water, makeup, or cleaning products.	Take the filtered, organic, or natural route when possible.
13 Having expectations of perfec-tion from yourself or imposed on you by others.	Be gentle and compassionate with yourself and surround yourself with people who have realistic expectations.

Think of these solutions as loving self-care methods that can gently steer you away from feeling frazzled and toward feeling grounded.

Adopt Routines to Calm Your Sensitive System

Routine is calming to the human nervous system, which partly is why small children can become cranky when their routines—like naptimes or mealtimes—are disrupted. Because empaths' hyper-perceptive nervous and energetic systems are easily overstimulated, routines are especially calming and stabilizing.

For this exercise, adopt daily morning, afternoon, and evening routines that make you feel grounded. Develop at least one routine—like the activities you do when you wake or right before bed—that you follow faithfully for a week. Switch up the details of some of your established routines to prevent boredom. Experiment and use these suggestions for inspiration!

MORNING ROUTINE SUGGESTIONS:

- If you struggle to find time for breakfast in the morning, make/have easy-to-prepare and healthy go-to breakfasts, like a smoothie or grain/nut bar.

- Take any necessary supplements or medication.

- Do something meditative alone to ground in to your own energy: walk; hit the gym; meditate; journal; draw an oracle card; or savor your morning coffee, tea, or kombucha on the porch.

- Allow yourself time to get ready so you don't feel rushed getting out the door.

- Choose an affirmation for the day to set the energetic tone, like "Life is supporting me in unexpected ways today" or "I'll show myself unconditional love today." Find daily affirmations in my calendar, *A Year of Self-Love.*

- Listen to upbeat, fun music if you're excited about the day or soothing music if you're stressed.

- Make your bed.

- Quickly straighten up the house so you'll be in, or return home to, a calmer environment.

AFTERNOON ROUTINE SUGGESTIONS:

- Avoid overscheduling and allow for transition time between activities.

- Eat something healthy that will boost your energy in the afternoon slump.

- Drink water or a noncaffeinated beverage without sugar.

- Get outside if you've been inside all day.

- Do something fun to uplift your energy and de-stress, like watching a silly video online, checking a social media feed that's generally positive or connecting, taking a pet or child for a walk, or chatting with a favorite coworker about something outside of work.

- Take a real lunch break for at least 20 to 30 minutes and don't check work email, pick up after children, or answer your work phone.

- Complete any tasks that must be done by the end of the day with time to spare so you don't feel rushed wrapping up.

EVENING ROUTINE SUGGESTIONS:

- Change into comfy clothes if you've been dressed up for work.

- Do something physical yet gentle to signal to your body that you're transitioning out of the daytime active mode and into evening relaxation mode, like leisurely strolling through the neighborhood with your spouse or roommate, playing your favorite music while prepping dinner, or getting down on the floor and playing with your child or pet.

- Get quiet time alone for 45 minutes. If you have kids or are a caregiver, this time might come at the end of the night when everyone else is in bed or relaxing in their own rooms.

- Work on a creative project that's just for fun for an hour. If you're a dancer, you might practice new moves. If you're an artist or crafter, you might spend an hour using your hands to make something beautiful.

- Avoid consuming too much alcohol or sugar. Be present with yourself as you prepare the evening meal (for example, notice the sounds and smells you experience as you cut veggies or strain noodles).

- Say a blessing over the meal, either silently or out loud, that involves gratitude.

- Make sure chores like washing dishes, taking out the trash, putting away laundry, and straightening are done so you wake up to a calm house tomorrow.

- Snuggle up—with pillows, your pet, your child, or your partner—to feel cozy.

- Try going to bed at roughly the same time every night.

- For an hour before bed, engage in low-stimulation activities like reading, journaling, stretching, or tidying the house. Avoid paying bills, watching the news, confrontations with family and roommates, or anything else that might put your system on alert.

Work with an Empath Talisman

Many faiths and cultures believe in the energy of sacred objects, and you probably already possess objects you consider sacred. Empaths can use these objects to help re-ground themselves when they are emotionally triggered, or experiencing an intense emotional reaction to something—a comment someone makes, an event that happens, or anything else. An old wound (like childhood abandonment) might get triggered, or maybe an ethical issue you believe in passionately is triggered.

Because emotions and energies can register strongly in an empath's system, when they're emotionally triggered, it might be challenging to stay centered in the present moment. You could come home after an emotionally triggering day and hold your empath talisman while unpacking your day with a friend on the phone, or you might keep your empath talisman in your pocket during an emotionally triggering situation, like confronting a coworker.

In the following exercise, you'll identify an empath talisman and infuse it with grounding energy.

1. Seek out your talisman, knowing that it may find you—this is how power objects are often discovered in shamanic traditions. You might be walking the beach and have one particular shell catch your eye, or you could walk into a store and feel one particular crystal calling to you. You can use an object already in your possession that you consider sacred, like a heart-shaped stone a child gave you or mala beads you bought while on a spiritual retreat.

2. Clear the energy of the object first, if you like, by giving it a gentle physical clean, leaving it out in the sunlight (provided that won't damage the object) or moonlight, or covering it in flower petals. Charge/infuse the object with grounding energy by holding

it between your hands, taking some deep breaths, and picturing in your mind a place (perhaps associated with an elder or ancient energy) where you often feel/felt grounded (your grandma's kitchen, an ancestral or sacred site you've visited). If there's an older tree you love, sit with the object under that tree, asking the tree and its roots to charge your talisman with grounding energy.

3. Practice working with and get to know your empath talisman. You might hold it while you meditate in the morning or wear it (if it's a piece of jewelry) while you attend a self-care workshop. Connect with its supportive energy and notice any changes in your own energy when you work with it. Name the changes, like feeling more calm, empowered, or open. Having something tactile that represents a feeling of being centered can help when you are emotionally triggered. An empath talisman can be a powerful self-care tool, yet not a substitute for other methods of getting emotional support. Work your talisman into the other healthy practices that keep you grounded.

Pick a Spirit Animal to Journey With

Spirit animals act as the embodiment of certain attractive traits a specific animal symbolizes that you might like to emulate. Spirit animals are empowering and fun to engage with. This exercise contains a list of spirit animals that can be especially valuable to empaths.

1. Read through the following descriptions and feel in to which animal would support you most now. Also, watch for synchronicities showing up in your life, such as seeing a certain animal in your yard, on social media, on a friend's T-shirt or mug, or in the news. You may even dream of an animal. The following suggests how spirit animals might help empaths.

   - **Cat:** Prioritizing healthy alone time.

   - **Dog:** Staying loyal to your own perspective.

   - **Duck:** Remaining adaptable to different types of energies, environments, and situations.

   - **Eagle:** Rising above the emotions and energies around you for a more objective perspective.

   - **Flamingo:** Feeling safe to be fabulous even if it upsets or threatens another.

   - **Groundhog:** Handling earthy needs and details.

   - **Horse:** Releasing another energetically so both of you can be free.

   - **Kangaroo:** Practicing exceptional self-care and self-nurturing.

   - **Owl:** Not letting others talk you out of your own wisdom.

- **Rabbit:** Taking care of your sensitive nervous and energetic systems.

- **Seal:** Cultivating a community of other empaths.

- **Stag:** Standing silently yet strongly in your own power and energy.

- **Turtle:** Coming home to your own energy, retreating and recovering.

- **Unicorn:** Celebrating what is unique about you, like being an empath!

2. Incorporate this spirit animal into your life by putting a figurine of this animal on your home altar, setting a screensaver image of this animal on your computer or phone, watching a documentary about this animal, contributing to a charity devoted to this animal, or meditating on an image of this animal.

Allow this animal to move your spirit, encouraging you to make positive changes in your self-care.

Bathe to Connect to
Your Higher Self and Intuition

Some empaths feel very at home in water! Immersing in a comfortable bathtub can be an ideal way to re-ground yourself and connect with both your physical and energy bodies. This ritual can also be a method of banking/conserving and increasing your energy!

Taking a bath is relaxing, and a relaxed state can facilitate getting in touch with your higher self. Your higher self is the part of you that is wise, reflective, and objective. It's the part of you that can feel your emotions but also create healthy distance from them. Your higher self is excellent at seeing the big picture and putting things into perspective. Like an eagle, it can fly high above the details of your daily life and look at things from a broader angle. You might consider the higher self the soul's perspective or wisdom.

Before you begin, schedule some time in a bathroom where you can close the door and be alone for 30 minutes. Then draw yourself a bath with water at a comfortable temperature, letting your mind quiet and enter a meditative state as you watch the tub fill up. Slip carefully inside and follow these steps.

1. Try to be fully present in the moment by engaging your senses. Use bath salts to make the water softer; sprinkle a few drops of lavender essential oil to create a sweet smell; if there's a safe spot to set a candle, light one with a glow you can gaze at; and/or put on some soothing nature sounds, music by an artist you love, or an inspirational podcast.

2. Connect with yourself. Take a few deep breaths, close your eyes for a few moments to center yourself, place your hand on your heart chakra, and gently splash some water over your arms and shoulders. Get a sense of your own amazing, powerful, strong energy!

3. Just be here with yourself, with minimal distractions, for 15, 20, 30 minutes, or longer. Let your mind go blank or quiet. If you have a favorite soap or gentle scrub, lovingly go over your skin and lather up.

4. Use this quiet, meditative time during which you can ground in to your own energy to naturally help you connect to your higher self. You might feel the energy change around you as you connect more to that part of yourself, which you could picture as an eagle or any mental image of wisdom. Expect some intuitive insights as well as some emotions to come up—perhaps about a current situation in your life or even something from the past. Notice what shows up now and trust that it's information coming from your higher self.

5. Repeat some affirming thoughts as you carefully get out of the tub and towel yourself off, like "I love this body" or "I'm learning to love this body."

When you're finished, be sure to fully extinguish any candles or incense you used in the ritual. If you don't have access to a bathtub, try a variation of this ritual in the shower.

Find Healthy Ways to Retreat

When you retreat, or pull back from overstimulating situations and the energies and emotions of others to ground back in to yourself, your sensitive nervous and energetic systems can recover. During healthy retreat and recovery, an empath can rest and rebalance, then emerge refreshed, centered, and excited to engage more actively with the world again.

Rate the following healthy retreat techniques that you've already tried as *excellent*, *okay*, or *not for me*, based on their ability to help your sensitive system recover. Then try at least one new technique.

_____ **Meditate at work.** If you have a door on your office, shut it to meditate. If you work in an open-office setting, take a walk on your lunch break or sit in a coffee shop after the lunch rush with your earbuds in to quiet your mind. If you work from home, try meditating on a park bench or your back porch.

_____ **Curl up with a good book.** Watching a film or listening to a podcast is also relaxing, but it's more stimulating. This is why reading is a great activity right before bed.

_____ **Spend time in a quiet spot in nature or gardening in the backyard.** Your child's Little League game may be held in a beautiful park, but it's hardly a low-stimulation environment! Look for relaxing spots instead.

_____ **Get lost in a fun creative project.** Have you been knitting so long that your hands just know what to do automatically? Maybe you can whip up a gourmet meal without having to think hard about it.

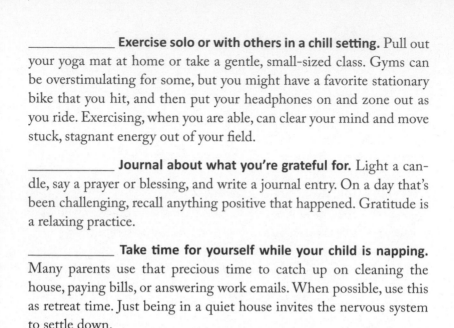

_____ **Exercise solo or with others in a chill setting.** Pull out your yoga mat at home or take a gentle, small-sized class. Gyms can be overstimulating for some, but you might have a favorite stationary bike that you hit, and then put your headphones on and zone out as you ride. Exercising, when you are able, can clear your mind and move stuck, stagnant energy out of your field.

_____ **Journal about what you're grateful for.** Light a candle, say a prayer or blessing, and write a journal entry. On a day that's been challenging, recall anything positive that happened. Gratitude is a relaxing practice.

_____ **Take time for yourself while your child is napping.** Many parents use that precious time to catch up on cleaning the house, paying bills, or answering work emails. When possible, use this as retreat time. Just being in a quiet house invites the nervous system to settle down.

_____ **Attend a contemplative spiritual service.** I once had a client who was not an Episcopalian yet would attend a weekly evening prayer service at an Episcopal chapel near her home because the church looked lovely lit up with candles and the choir sang soothing music. Many spiritual traditions offer similar services that are often open to the public.

_____ **Do a group project where everyone is quietly working.** This might be a crafting hour with your kids on the weekends or a writing group that meets to work side by side yet silently at a coffee shop. You don't necessarily have to be alone to enjoy retreat-and-recover time.

The ideas listed in this exercise, or others like them, will help your sensitive system get the space and quiet time it needs to retreat and recover in an intentional way.

QUIZ: Are You Retreating in a Healthy Way or Isolating and Numbing Out?

Every empath has their own preferences for how much retreat time they like, based on their individual personalities and current life circumstances. If you're going through an unusually stressful period, for example, it might be beneficial to have a bit more retreat time. But be careful not to go so far as to isolate yourself.

For an empath—who is wired to interact so intimately with others—feeling isolated from the outside world is just as draining as being overstimulated by it. Numbing out due to chronic overstimulation can look like mindless binge-watching, compulsive shopping, or heavy drinking, to offer a few examples. These behaviors could be an empath's way of attempting to block out what they're absorbing from others or feeling in themselves.

To see if your retreat is healthy or isolating/numbing, answer the following quiz questions with a simple *yes*, *no*, or *sometimes*. Keep in mind that there are no wrong answers to this quiz and no pass or fail grading. It's simply a way to get clear on your current retreat-and-recover methods.

_____ Is my retreat-and-recover time defined, so I know when I'm engaging in it, how long it lasts, and how often I need it?

_____ Is my retreat-and-recover time filled with activities that are enjoyable, nurturing, and don't produce feelings of guilt?

_____ Do I feel refreshed and motivated to re-engage with the world again after healthy retreat-and-recover time?

_____ Am I periodically switching up the activities involved in my retreat-and-recover time so I don't get bored?

_____ Can I find ways to retreat and recover when I'm still around others, like coloring quietly beside my partner while they're on the computer, or snuggling with a pet while I watch a movie?

_____ Am I comfortable being alone with myself and do I enjoy my own company? (Practice radical self-love and acceptance when gently contemplating this question.)

_____ Do I have people I can talk to when I'm upset, so retreating isn't my only coping skill when I'm worked up?

_____ Was I taught as a child, or was it modeled for me, that retreat or alone time can be healthy and nourishing?

_____ Do I generally feel better after retreat time?

_____ Do I retreat because it's healthy and not because I experience uncomfortable social anxiety when I'm around others?

The more *yes* answers you had, the more your current retreat-and-recover strategy is working for you. If you had a lot of *no* answers, talk to a healthcare professional, counselor, or trusted friend about ways you can make healthy changes. Loved ones (especially those who also seem sensitive, like other empaths) who are good at staying centered and calm might be able to share how they retreat and recover. Their methods could give you some inspiration!

Identify Gentle and Enlivening Activities to Adjust Your Energy

One of the bonuses of being sensitive to energy is that empaths may be able to more easily adjust their own energy simply by seeking out activities, people, or places with an energy they want to experience.

Gentle activities are ideal for when you're anxious, drained, or very emotional. When you want to calm your energy, try:

- Strolling or taking a slow-moving yoga class.
- Hanging with a friend who has a very laid-back energy.
- Visiting a quiet museum, bookstore, or spiritual retreat center.
- Sitting at a café off the beaten path during its slow time of day.
- Doing your grocery shopping when you're not rushed and the store isn't crowded.
- Getting a relaxing massage or nontoxic/organic pedicure.
- Sitting and holding hands with someone on a park bench or watching the sunset.
- Daydreaming.

Enlivening activities are great for when you're bored or wanting to feel more connected, alive, or energized. (While empaths may be more easily overstimulated than others, they still enjoy feeling excited and engaged with life and sometimes crave higher-stimulation activities.) Those include:

- Falling in love with a person, a project, yourself, or life itself.
- Hanging with a friend who has bubbly, outgoing energy.
- Attending a concert, sporting event, peaceful protest, or celebration in a crowd of engaged people.
- Having an intense workout.
- Learning or trying something new.

- Attending a class in a group setting (remotely or in person).
- Dancing around in a silly or joyous way.
- Being around someone who is inspired and motivated.
- Setting goals that make you stretch toward your dreams or overcome obstacles.
- Performing or speaking in front of others.
- Making big changes that feel right, like moving or switching jobs (or even planning such a change).

Staying in touch with your own energy helps you discern which type of activity is best for you at any given time.

Take Your System Off Red Alert

Because empaths are naturally built to feel so much, they can feel things very intensely. When you're feeling good stuff, like being deeply connected to others or nature, you're enjoying one of the best parts of being an empath. When you're feeling painful things, like the collective anxiety of others, however, you're experiencing one of the most challenging parts of being an empath.

If you're dealing with temporary, circumstantial stress, and you're feeling it in an intense way, try some of the following techniques to take your system off red alert.

- **Cushion with buffer.** Your system is telling you it's overloaded, so create more buffer around yourself. Buffer could look like scheduling a massage, attending a yoga class twice instead of once a week, or some other way of mindfully increasing your self-care to create buffer. When you feel on red alert or very anxious, it's as if you are a car and the shocks or brake pads are worn too thin. Buffer is protective cushioning inserted into your schedule to help calm you and to soften or take the edge off daily life.

- **Let go of some responsibilities temporarily or create open space in your immediate-future schedule.** You may be doing too much now, and managing everything is creating the overwhelm. Empaths need retreat-and-recover time to re-ground, and if you're so busy you're not getting that downtime, it could quickly lead to feeling on red alert. Create space and let your system catch up.

- **Make some bigger changes in your life.** Are you people-pleasing and not prioritizing yourself? Are you taking on too much because you, not others, are expecting too much of yourself? Even if what's causing you to be on red alert is a temporary issue, it could be helping you see some deeper truths or patterns that are reaching a crisis point. Empaths are extrasensory but not superhuman!

- **Slow down.** As a society, we're frequently impatient and on red alert. Are you ever moving quickly when you don't have to be, or rushing through errands or conversations or projects simply because you've gotten used to moving very fast? Walk slower, talk slower—eat slower! This technique helps quiet your mind too.

These techniques work for sporadic stress. Feeling overwhelmed almost all the time, however, might lead to a chronic fight-flight-or-freeze response. When you enter this territory, the adrenals and other systems in your body go on red alert, and in a primal way that makes you feel unsafe. Animals in the forest may feel this way if they smell a fire, for example.

If you're feeling anxiety and panic on a regular basis, talk to a healthcare professional. A counselor can give you coping skills or determine if this is related to a past trauma; a doctor, nurse practitioner, or naturopath can help determine if there is a physical cause; and a psychiatrist can help determine if there is a brain chemistry issue. Get any support you need so you can savor life more again!

Bless Your Meals

Small, easy rituals throughout the day help empaths mindfully ground back in to their own energy, keeping them centered and calmer. The beginning of a meal—whether it's dinner or just a quick snack at your desk—is the perfect excuse to stop and perform a simple ritual.

The following is a sample for a blessing you can perform over any meal, whether you're at home or in a restaurant, eating alone or sitting with a group of people. Use these steps as a guideline, but feel free to adapt them to your preferences.

1. Express (silently or aloud) gratitude for this food and the life force it's transferring to you. If you consume animal products, you could thank the animals for what they have contributed. If you are on a plant-based diet, remember to thank them for their nutrients. Don't forget to thank humans, like farmers or the people who work at your grocery store. You can even thank the person who earned the money to buy this food—maybe that was you!

2. Set the intention to use this food as fuel to love yourself, to be of service to others, to spread compassion in the world, or for any other noble intention that resonates. (Again, this can be communicated aloud or silently.)

3. Begin your meal, and let the sacredness of this quick and easy ritual make you more mindful of the blessing of having healthy food. Feeling blessed is the best!

Tune In to Why You're Feeling Ungrounded

A healthy self-care practice is the best way to feel grounded—or safe, confident, calm, and centered in your own energy. If you're feeling ungrounded—consistently feeling scattered, unsafe, insecure, or anxious—lean in to any self-care techniques that are especially supportive for you or for empaths in general.

For this exercise, you'll be using your clairsentient psychic pathway to feel in to the possible reasons why you may not be grounded. Ask yourself the following questions, and don't go to your logical mind to deduce or strategize the answer. Wait for your feelings to tell you which questions hold important clues for you now.

When a question resonates as possibly true for you, the energy around you might feel heavier or thicker; you might experience physical sensations, like chills; or you might experience any other mild physical or energetic change, like a wave of energy or emotion washing over you. When you read a question from the following list and it doesn't resonate as an issue for you, you won't experience a physical or energetic change, and instead you will feel neutral about or uninterested in this particular issue.

Are you feeling ungrounded because:

- The future feels particularly uncertain (where you'll go to school, where you'll live, where you'll work) and you're having trouble being at peace with this uncertain future?

- You don't feel settled in a home, job, or relationship that is new or in a transition period?

- You're having real concerns about survival issues, like food, shelter, physical safety, or other survival needs being met?

- You have not had enough time or space to connect with yourself and come home to your own energy?

- There's too much pressure being put on you right now, either by yourself, a boss, a friend, or a partner, and instead of just being an extrasensory empath you're trying to be superhuman?

- You haven't spent time in nature recently?

- You haven't been sticking to a healthy diet or you haven't been taking supplements and medication that you know work for you?

- You are trying to go it alone and need to ask for support?

- You've been numbing out a lot and aren't being present enough in the moment?

- There's something coming up that needs to be looked at and healed, either from the recent or distant past, and you need to get support and tools to face it?

- You're staying busy to avoid your emotions, an issue, or a person?

- You're being rigid and inflexible, even about smaller issues? Is this because you feel out of control in some area of your life and are trying to exert control in another area?

- You haven't been sticking to a healthy routine?

You don't have to possess magical solutions for any of these issues. Simply getting in touch with what is making you feel ungrounded will help you tune in to your own emotions and energies, and that in itself always helps an empath feel more grounded. If anything you discover in this exercise upsets you or makes you want to change, get support from loved ones and experts. Seeking help can be an act of courage, wisdom, and self-love.

Try Beauty Therapy

Whether you're experiencing joyous times or very tough times, beauty is a sustaining, nourishing force for the human spirit. Beauty can instantly create warm, positive emotions, like joy, peace, and even awe. Because empaths are sensitive to emotions, beauty therapy helps them quickly tune in to feel-good vibes. For one week, commit to bringing more beauty into your life or noticing the beauty already there.

- **Day One:** Find beauty in unexpected places, like a gnarled tree trunk or the tears of someone grieving a loved one.

- **Day Two:** Concentrate on feeling more beautiful, like wearing your favorite outfit or having an attitude that radiates beauty.

- **Day Three:** Bring more beauty to your workspace, like clearing clutter from your desk or placing a small plant or crystal on it.

- **Day Four:** Notice the beauty in other people, like the kind smile of a stranger or the warm, nurturing energy of a close friend.

- **Day Five:** Bring more beauty to your home, like buying a lovely vase at a secondhand store or purchasing one on sale at a chic store, or listening to beautiful music and letting it fill your space.

- **Day Six:** Breathe in the beauty of nature, like visiting a local park for fresh air or burning sweet-smelling natural incense.

- **Day Seven:** Make a meal beautiful, like creating a restaurant-level presentation of your dinner or using different vegetable shapes and colors in a salad.

Beauty therapy does not have to cost a lot of, or even any, money. Sensitive empaths pick up easily on subtleties in their environment, so a little beauty therapy goes a long way.

CHAPTER 3

Mindfully Tune In and Out of Other People

An empath's default wiring is to tune in to what's around them—the energies and emotions of other individuals, groups, and spaces. Yet it's important to remember that you are not at the mercy of this sensitivity—at least not all the time! You can learn to mindfully tune in and out of others, and while this is not a perfect science, it's an ability you can practice and hone using the techniques in this chapter.

Many empaths have a fear of being drained by other people's energies and emotions. Sometimes this fear can protect you, and other times it can hold you back. While you should not feel victimized by being an empath, protecting yourself is a legitimate concern. So is feeling free to pursue things you'd like to experience.

To understand this concept, visualize a knob on a panel that's labeled *empath sensitivity*. This chapter will help you get better at turning your sensitivity up or down. The key to managing your intake of others' energies and emotions is to turn the knob toward *observer mode* when helpful. Other times, the dial will point more toward *opening up to feel* so you can actively engage and enjoy your sensitivity. While you'll have more control in some situations than in others, you can usually do *something* to mindfully manage your sensitivity. At times you'll want to let the moment organically dictate your response and not think about your dial at all. The techniques in this chapter provide tools to manage your empath sensitivity in an empowered way.

Tune In for Intuitive Insight

Focusing on another person can enable you to tune in to them in a powerful way. Before an intuitive session, I focus on my client—what I know about them if we've had a session before, and the questions they sent me to meditate on. Within seconds of turning my thoughts and full attention on them, I start getting insightful intuitive hits about my client via the four main psychic pathways (hearing, seeing, knowing, and feeling).

The following exercise will help you practice focusing—on people, situations, or anything else—so you can gain more intuitive insight. Learning what it feels like to tune in and tune out (which we'll cover soon) are vital self-care lessons for empaths so they can decide which is the most useful and healthy option for them in the moment.

1. **Decide what you want to practice focusing on.** It might be your pet as you play together, or your coworker over lunch as she asks for your advice. It could be someone or something far away, like a lover who's asleep on the other side of the world or a vacation spot your family is considering. You might also focus on a situation, like how you want to grow or adapt your business next year.

2. **Get comfortable.** Take care of any physical concerns so you're not distracted. Go to the bathroom, grab a snack, or get settled in your chair.

3. **Stay calm.** Remind yourself that this is not the type of focus used when cramming for an exam. Your energy should feel soft and open, not intense and concentrated. Gently let everything except what you are focusing on fade away.

4. **Encourage your focus.** If you're researching vacation spots, pull up images online. If you're focusing on a friend across the table, make eye contact and notice the details of their outfit. If a stray thought about something else enters (such as "What's for dinner?" or "Did I send that email?"), let it float on by. If it's important, it will resurface after the exercise.

5. **Notice what intuitive hits you're getting.** Observe the words you hear in your mind, thoughts you have, images you see in your mind, and feelings you experience that are related to what you're focusing on.

6. **Transition your focus.** To end the exercise, mindfully take your focus and your thoughts somewhere else. Give your system a break, and if any essential intuitive insights still want to pop in, they will.

Use Focus with a Sensitive Friend

This exercise provides another way to practice using focus for intuitive insight. If you have another sensitive friend with a naturally strong or open intuition, it can be a special bonding experience to try the following exercise together. It might become something you do periodically whenever one of you is looking for some out-of-the-box intuitive insight on a situation in your life. Always trust your own guidance, of course—but going to someone else for their intuitive opinion can be enlightening, especially if you're feeling very emotional or stuck around an issue in your life.

Before you begin, find a friend who is excited about trying this. If they're not familiar with the four psychic pathways, or "clairs," explain the concept of hearing, seeing, knowing, or feeling intuitive guidance. After you've set up a time to meet, either in person or over the phone, do the following.

1. Decide who will be the first subject of focus, you or your friend.

2. Decide what issue you will be focusing on. (For example, you could decide to focus on your friend first, and the issue is a challenge he's currently having in a romantic relationship.) For this exercise, pick a situation that isn't too emotionally loaded for your friend. Concentrate instead on something merely annoying or frustrating (like how his partner has been working too much lately). This keeps the exercise fun and your energy light and curious.

3. Encourage focus by clearing your mind of anything else and turning your thoughts and full attention to your friend and his issue for 15 to 20 minutes. If you're meeting in person, notice his outfit and facial expressions. If you're on the phone, concentrate on his voice. Ask your friend to share what's going on by giving you some

details of the situation. Give your friend space to process some of his emotions, frustrations, or confusion aloud.

4. Listen between the lines. As you listen to your friend, also pay attention to what insightful thoughts pop into your head about his situation or what feelings you experience about it. For example, you might have a thought that your friend's partner is trying to prove himself at work right now yet it's tied to fears about a job loss he experienced in the distant past, or get a feeling that an idea your friend has about how to address the issue is a good one. You might even see things, like the face of a family member of yours who went through something similar, pop into your head, or hear things, like "This is a special love," when your friend talks about his partner.

5. Share what you are sensing about your friend's situation with him as natural openings in the conversation occur. (If you think something you picked up might upset your friend, or you're not sure if something is helpful advice or not, don't share it yet. Go away from the exercise and sit on it for a few days.) Stick to advice that's inspirational and practical and expressed in a way that is loving. Remember: You're not trying to tell your friend what to do or fix his life—just diplomatically offering suggestions and practicing mindfully tuning in to others.

6. When you're done, repeat the process but reverse things so you and one of your issues becomes the focus.

Take Your Focus Off Someone Who Is Triggering

Certain people might be particularly distracting, because what they say, do, or represent to you is so triggering. These people can appear in any facet of your life, like a coworker who dominates meetings or a well-meaning neighbor who always offers unwanted advice. You might even find someone in the public eye, like a Hollywood celebrity or politician, triggering.

The following protocol for dealing with a triggering person can be illuminating for empaths, and after trying this method, you may find your energy refreshed or your relationship with this triggering person improved.

1. **Admit that someone is triggering you.** Instead of downplaying their effect on you, just get honest with yourself and maybe even someone else who is safe to confide in about how much this person's energy and presence is getting under your empath skin. Remember that you're sensitive to the energies of others, so finding yourself in this situation occasionally is natural.

2. **Identify why this person triggers you.** For example, an acquaintance might like to gossip, and you hate hearing them speak poorly about other people. Or someone you like and admire might have suddenly become triggering because they got married, landed their dream job, or got out of debt and it's making you a bit jealous because you'd love something similar.

3. **Determine what this trigger is telling you.** When you are having trouble tuning out of someone, it might be because your sensitive energy body is trying to get your attention. What do you need to see here that this person represents? It could be that you should have better boundaries with your loved ones, for example, or that

there's a goal this person has achieved that you'd like to go after in your own way. Ponder what this person's triggering energy is inviting you to do—often it involves some type of healing. For example, it might be that this person reminds you of something painful from the past that needs more healing. Feel the feelings, and discern the messages within them.

4. **Take action.** What can you do about what you discovered in the previous step? Once you set better boundaries or start going after a dream (or let it go and count your other blessings instead), or simply process emotions that want to be felt, this person's energy should become less triggering and it will be much easier to tune them out. Sometimes simply realizing why they trigger you and admitting it to yourself is the most helpful action.

5. **Turn your thoughts elsewhere.** When this person isn't around, try not thinking about them, unless the thoughts are productive and related to the third and fourth steps. Sometimes we cannot avoid being around someone—like a coworker, neighbor, or an extended family member—yet we can certainly work on not thinking about them when our time around them is over. Thinking about someone, or not, is a powerful way to tune in or out of that person's energy. If thinking of them has become a habit, start a new habit of switching to thoughts about gratitude when this person comes to mind.

A good self-care practice will sometimes ask you to explore your inconvenient or even painful emotions. Be very gentle and loving with yourself as you enter this vulnerable territory, and get any extra support you need. Know that positive change and healing can be the results.

Practice Observer Mode and Witnessing Energy

Empaths have a special place inside they can retreat to, even when they're around many people. Entering observer mode and witnessing others allows you to enjoy or support the person you're around without feeling that person's energies or emotions intimately. Witnessing is one of the most useful techniques in an empath's self-care kit.

There will be times when someone else's energies and emotions overtake you regardless of your best efforts. But your best efforts will help significantly, and get even better with time and practice. The more you mindfully work with observer mode, the more your own systems will automatically switch into observer mode when the situation calls for it.

You'll know you are in observer mode when you are:

- Pulling back into your own energy. You might imagine that your energy body is a cape or cloak, which can be open and unfurled when you want to open up and feel. In observer mode, you will pull your energy back, like wrapping that same cape or cloak around you instead. Get a mental image of your energy cape or cloak—is it bold like a superhero's, or is it simple and understated, or decorated with intricate, colorful embroidery?

- Witnessing someone else's energies and emotions with concern or pleasure but also with curiosity. Instead of wanting to relate to them, feel with them, or change their emotion, you are lovingly allowing them the space to feel and process their emotions, both the wonderful ones and the challenging ones.

- Mimicking the energy of people you know who are adept at using witnessing energy. Doctors and counselors can be excellent at it because it allows them to use critical thinking and observation to better diagnose and help patients—instead of becoming overwhelmed by their patients' emotions. Doctors and counselors may be tuning in to you emotionally, but they have real boundaries and conditions with that.

- Experiencing a balanced emotional state or energy, even as those around you are experiencing big emotions, like joy, anxiety, grief, or eager anticipation. In observer mode, you are surfing on top of and around these emotional waves while balancing on your own sturdy, stable energy.

- Imagining space between your energy body and someone else's, or imagining your energy body shrinking back into your physical body as if your physical body is a shield. Witnessing energy is holding someone else's energy at arm's length, no matter how close they are to you physically, creating neutral, open energetic space between you.

Sometime in the next few days, practice mindfully entering observer mode—perhaps when your partner comes home filled with intense energy and tells you about an amazing day at work, or when your child cries over a friend who's hurt their feelings, or when you see something on the news that troubles you. You can take action to help others or simply offer comfort while in observer mode. In fact, you might find you have more stamina for supporting others when you are engaging witnessing energy.

Using witnessing energy does not mean you stop caring, or become cold. Empaths can still have great compassion for others without feeling all their energies and emotions quite so intimately. Sometimes holding a calm space for someone who is very emotional is the most loving action.

Open Up to Feel

Sometimes as an empath, you will want to open up to feel more and mindfully encourage your amazing ability to sense the energies and emotions of others. This practice can allow you to experience bliss, like celebrating a dear friend who got a dream job, or a family member who got sober. There are even times when you might want to open up to feel the challenging, painful emotions and energies of others.

Opening up to feel in to suffering on the other side of the world can inform your actions, like inspiring you to make a charitable donation, volunteer, change the way you vote, or change the way you shop. Other times, feeling the suffering of someone else might give you a clearer window into your own suffering or make you feel less alone in the struggles of human existence. Opening up to feel challenging things can also simply be a way to authentically honor who you are, an empath, as well as honor the person who is suffering by being with them energetically in an intimate way.

Opening up to feel and mindfully using your empath ability feels like:

- Your own energetic and emotional systems are active and tingly. You might feel the energy around you or in you change, like becoming thicker or lighter. *Any* change or palpable shift in the energy around you or inside yourself means you have opened up to feel more. Your emotions may change as well, like feeling sad or happy or anything else that the person you are tuning in to is feeling.

- Your heart chakra and heart energy are awakened. This is what the phrase "My heart goes out to you" is describing. Your heart energy can make you feel very compassionate; tender; emotionally receptive; and moved to help, comfort, or connect with someone.

- Having knowledge of what someone else is feeling because you are feeling it too through clairsentience, as opposed to having that knowledge come another way, like via the intellectual psychic pathway of claircognizance as a breakthrough thought, strong knowing, or mental download.

- Experiencing physical changes related to what someone else is feeling, like tearing up if they are very sad or noticing your eyes widen and smile broaden if they are very happy.

- Your emotions and energy body still buzzing or feeling more engaged, even if just briefly, after you have stopped tuning in or ended your interaction with this person.

Sometime in the next week, practice mindfully opening up to feel. You can practice letting your heart go out to a loved one or coworker, or to an issue in the larger world. Notice if you feel any of the sensations noted here.

Opening up to feel is a dynamic way to connect with others, but it is also a dynamic way to connect with yourself and your empath ability. In that sense, opening up to feel more is an act of self-care and self-love.

Process Your Emotions Before Using Witnessing Energy

Observer mode and witnessing energy are not meant to be used as an emotional bypass that helps you avoid your own feelings. In fact, if you try to use observer mode to protect yourself before you process your strong emotions, it won't work well. This protocol *does* work well for situations when you know in advance that you'll face a triggering person or situation and you want to meet them/it in observer mode to minimize drama, protect your sensitive empath system, or support someone who is going through an emotional time.

You might encounter a situation when you should process your own emotions before you use observer mode if, for example, a close friend is ill and you want to be strong and supportive for them; a triggering family member will be at an upcoming event and you want to keep the peace; you're very jealous of someone but want to celebrate their win with them in a loving way; or you know your win will be difficult for someone you love and you want to share your good news with them in a more subdued or neutral way (imagine you win an Oscar but your bestie isn't even nominated). Here's how.

1. Acknowledge your emotions. It can help to name these emotions—"I'm sad" or "I'm excited," for instance—but don't judge them as right or wrong, good or bad.

2. Find a healthy way to process these emotions. Refer back to the Develop a Personalized Method to Process Your Emotions exercise in Chapter 2.

3. Pay special attention to the processing technique of sharing your emotions with someone. Pick someone safe, loving, and discreet who isn't too close to the situation.

4. If possible, wait to enter observer mode until your emotions have cooled. For example, wait until the situation doesn't seem so bad or even so intensely good, or until you can see fresh perspectives, you start to soften toward a person or situation that upset you, or you can think less emotionally and more objectively or practically. If it's *not* possible to wait to enter observer mode until your emotions have cooled, see the Enter Observer Mode Quickly exercise in this chapter.

Connecting with and processing your own emotions first clears space for you to fully embrace observer mode with an open mind and heart.

Switch Back and Forth Between
Observing and Feeling

Most of life exists in the gray areas or between extremes. Many times, especially with practice and understanding, you will be holding space with others by engaging *both* witnessing energy and your empath ability to open up and feel more, switching back and forth automatically between the two. You're looking for a balance.

If the balance feels too far to one extreme, lean back the other way. For example, if you're opening up to feel (whether you've made the mindful decision to do this or your own energetic and emotional systems have engaged on their own), but you start to become emotionally overwhelmed and drained, mindfully switch into observer mode. Sometimes when an empath is feeling generally run-down, it's a great time to practice leaning more toward witnessing energy to rebalance. On the other hand, if you're feeling isolated or disconnected, or you simply want to feel more intimately connected with someone, switch out of observer mode and open up to feel with heart energy.

Switching back and forth between witnessing energy and opening up to feel is something I do naturally in sessions with clients. You're no doubt doing the same in your own life. For this exercise, you'll simply be doing it more mindfully to help you get clear on what both approaches are like, as well as why and when you might switch back and forth.

Try to let this exercise occur organically. You don't have to plan for it ahead of time. Maybe after you read this section of the book, life will present you with the perfect opportunity to practice this exercise! Look for a situation where someone wants to share and confide in you about something that is upsetting them or something they're really excited about. A situation like this should not be hard to come by, as many empaths naturally attract this sort of deep sharing. Then follow these steps.

1. As the person begins telling you what they're upset or excited about, check in with yourself. Are you tired or anxious? If so, you might want to lead with witnessing energy, which can be less draining. Are you feeling bored or lonely, or has this other person already engaged your heart energy automatically? Perhaps opening up to feel more with your clairsentience will be nourishing or appropriate.

2. As the person keeps sharing and you engage with words of comfort or advice, or mirror back to them their own joy, check in with yourself about what you feel that person needs most. Would a grounded, calm witnessing energy help them ground or express and process emotions, or do you sense that letting your heart go out to them and feeling with them would make them feel more seen and less alone or strengthen/deepen your bond?

3. Once you decide mentally, or your energy and emotions decide naturally, which energy to lead with—witnessing or opening up to feel—notice how it becomes a dance, where at times you feel a tug on your own heart, and then at other times you pull back and snuggle into your own energy.

4. After the encounter ends, notice how witnessing in observer mode and opening up to feel are different. You may think of witnessing energy as intellectual and opening up to feel as emotional.

You will receive intuitive insights using both, so it's important to know that you don't have to choose one method over another. Keeping a balance of each will serve you well.

Enter Observer Mode Quickly

This exercise is perfect for everyday situations with people you interact with briefly or casually, like strangers standing next to you in line who may be throwing off some difficult or funky energies and emotions.

Follow these steps to practice getting into an observer frame of mind in just moments.

1. Quickly imagine the energy field that naturally surrounds your body as a cape or cloak. Imagine this magical garment any way you like: soft and comforting or flashy and runway ready. Now picture yourself drawing that energy cape or cloak very close around you. Or you can imagine your energy body pulling away from the other person so there is open space between the two of you. Or you can imagine your energy body shrinking back into your physical body as if your physical body is a shield.

2. As you notice the energies or emotions of this other person, name them in your mind (frustrated, bored, happy, anxious, sad, excited, confused, angry). As an empath, you might get extra intuitive data, like perhaps how this person's mood has to do with their frustrations about the future or an underlying loneliness.

3. Observe with curiosity how this person is feeling, but stay in your head instead of going into your heart. (Example: "Oh, that's interesting. This cashier seems a little bored and down. I'm getting the intuitive information that it's because there is something in her life outside of work she's unhappy about. I'll be sure to smile at her when she gives me my receipt. It has nothing to do with me, so I'll let these observations fade away as I walk out of the store.") These observations will probably come to you quickly as a mental

download, which means you are using the intellectual psychic pathway, claircognizance.

4. Take your attention somewhere else directly after your interaction. One of the most powerful ways we tune in to other people is simply by thinking about them. When you do not want to engage in their energy, though, it's important to take your mind to another subject or engage your body in an activity.

Practicing witnessing energy in these everyday situations will slowly give you the skills and confidence to practice observer mode when the emotional stakes are higher and more personal.

Your energy body is connected to your physical body, yet also larger than—and not limited to—the confines of the physical body. Empaths have a very sensitive energy body and naturally notice the changes in their own and other people's energy bodies.

List Ways to Connect with Your Unique Energy

If you're feeling scattered or drained by the energy of those around you or the larger world, a fun way to re-ground in to your own energy is to celebrate or emphasize the unique ways that you do you! The following list will help. Complete the statements, jotting your answers down here or writing them in your journal. Refer to this list whenever you need to feel more grounded.

- I love to spend a lazy day…

- The following causes are close to my heart…

- My ideal longer vacation involves…

- My ideal day trip is…

- My creative outlet is…

- When I'm scared, I typically comfort myself with…

- I'm most connected to my spirituality when…

- I feel most alive and on purpose when…

- I always feel centered and grounded by…

- Some of the things that are most unique about me are…

- I'd describe my sense of humor as…

- My favorite way to celebrate is…

- I express my love for people by…

- Some adjectives I would use to describe myself are…

- I adore dressing in…

- Some of the things I love most about myself are...

- People often compliment me on or admire me for...

- My biggest dreams and life goals include...

- I'm naturally good at...

- I've learned to be good at...

- My favorite foods are...

- My favorite musical artists are...

- My favorite nature settings include...

- My favorite ways to nurture or connect with my body are...

- I think part of the reason my soul is here is to

- Someone I talk to when I'm upset is...

- People I like to share my big and small wins with include...

- I am almost always cheered up by...

- Some of the things I'm most grateful for in my life are...

Tune In to the Energy of Nature

Empaths have a special relationship with nature, and strolling or sitting in nature at least once a week gives your energy body a tune-up. Seek out places where you feel immersed in nature, if possible. Before you start this exercise, locate a calm, immersive outdoor setting where you can ground in to your own energy—pick a spot where the vibes are chill and noise levels are relatively low. Allow at least 20 minutes, or even 30 to 45 minutes, alone for this exercise. Practice what you've learned in the other exercises in this chapter about tuning in and focusing—you want to achieve a gentle, soft focus, encouraging your sensitive energy body to open up and feel. To get started:

1. Take a few deep, calming breaths to get into your physical body and out of your mind. Whether you're sitting still on a park bench or strolling along a boardwalk, try to slow down your thoughts so that you experience fewer thoughts. Work with a mantra if that helps, like "I'm resting my mind for a bit."

2. Engage mindfully with your five physical senses. Are you smelling the damp dirt and moss of the forest floor? Do you hear a squirrel scampering through a bush as leaves shake loose behind it? You might be watching waves rush up to a beach's shore, or feeling the wet, grainy sand beneath your feet. If you're sipping water, coffee, or kombucha, notice how it tastes.

3. Observe how you feel. Do you feel less scattered? Ideally, you're experiencing relaxation now. If your mind is chattering or wandering, continue to try to notice your surroundings. If you're near trees, focus gently on the color of the leaves and the texture of the bark. Noticing the details of your environment will help your mind settle. Take more slow, deep breaths.

4. Determine if you are getting any signals from your energy body. You might feel physical sensations, like a lightening of your energy field, which will make your physical body feel less heavy—like floating in a pool. Or you might experience changes in your mood, like feeling generally calmer or happier. If you feel more alive, that's probably a signal you're more present in the moment than usual. Feeling more powerful? That's you being grounded, centered in your own energy.

5. Practice tuning in to some of the natural elements around you. You'll observe as you gently focus on a large mountain in the distance that its energy feels different than the rock at your feet. (Remember: You tune in to something or someone simply by focusing on it/them.) A wide open sky might make you feel more expansive, like life is full of possibility it is! Or the roots of a sturdy tree might make you feel more stable despite current life changes. Notice most of all how you are becoming one with the energy of all the nature around you. Now your energy is humming along peacefully, matched to a frequency it loves!

6. Notice any intuitive insights you receive. As you quiet your thinking mind, your sixth sense has more space to send you guidance. Watch for claircognizant thoughts that appear in your mind fully formed or as out-of-the-box solutions. You might have begun this exercise confused about a situation but get clarity via intuitive guidance by the end!

Some empaths insist they get their best intuitive "hits," or insights, outside. Nature is grounding, and when you're grounded it's easier to get guided! Yet remember your intuition is part of you. Connect more with yourself to increase intuitive hits anytime, anywhere.

Create More Space Between Your Thoughts

Psychologist and spiritual teacher Wayne Dyer described meditation as increasing the space between your thoughts. Sounds simple, doesn't it? Yet it can be quite challenging. I once attended a workshop where the teacher asked a roomful of people to try quieting their minds and counting the seconds between their thoughts. "I couldn't even count one second!" a woman said afterward, laughing. Whether you're a natural-born Buddha, or someone who naturally has a very active, chatty mind, sitting for 10 minutes and trying to expand the space between your thoughts will help you quiet your mind. Quieting your mind is a powerful way to center yourself, and from that more centered energetic place, you will have more control over mindfully tuning in or out of something or someone. If you do the following exercise every day for a full week or even a full month, you might be pleasantly surprised at the progress you make.

1. Pick a quiet spot to meditate alone where you won't be disturbed for 10 minutes.

2. Consider adding ambient noise to give your mind something to focus on, like the sound of rain or a white-noise machine.

3. Get seated in a comfortable position.

4. Now simply try to increase the quiet space between your thoughts so you have fewer thoughts for 5 to 10 minutes. Concentrate on your breath or the feel of your chair, for example.

5. Reward yourself, whatever the results, with loving thoughts for trying!

Meditation is like anything else—with patience and practice, you will improve.

Find Your Meditation Style

Meditating helps empaths reset their energy and train their brain to stop thinking of someone or something to tune back in to themselves. Try the following meditation styles to discern your favorites.

- **Traditional meditation:** Sit or lie in a comfortable position, close your eyes, and quiet your mind.

- **Guided meditation:** Listen to a recording of someone else or make a recording of yourself talking you through the meditation. Guided meditations may have themes, like connecting to a spirit guide.

- **Breath-work meditation:** Use mindful breathing, and concentration on your breath, to help the body and mind relax.

- **Sound meditation:** Give your mind something gentle to focus on—like the sound of chanting, nature, or healing music—to encourage it to quiet.

- **Walking meditation:** Engage in repetitive movement to calm or still the mind. Walking meditation is an ancient practice.

- **Creative meditation:** Immerse yourself in a creative project, like painting, sewing, or baking, to quiet the mind.

- **Everyday meditation:** Increase space between your thoughts while performing activities like shopping, cleaning, or showering.

- **Nature meditation:** Use the energy of nature—like being in nature or listening to nature sounds—to enter a meditative state.

- **Mantra meditation:** Replace scattered thoughts with a healing mantra, like "I'm discovering peace" or any other healing phrase.

If you have a meditation style, experiment with a new technique!

Determine If an Emotion Is Yours
or Someone Else's

When *anyone* is overwhelmed by a challenging emotion (like panic, sadness, or anger), it's always good to get clear on what this emotion is trying to convey, do something to help process the emotion in a safe way, and reach out for support. When an *empath* is overwhelmed by an emotion, that protocol is still important, yet the empath might add one crucial step first—asking themselves: "Is this emotion mine or someone else's?"

An overwhelming emotion might build slowly over days or weeks, or an overwhelming emotion may appear out of nowhere. When an empath is overwhelmed by a challenging emotion, a few things might be happening.

- You could be picking up on someone else's energies and emotions, like those of a loved one who is grieving.

- You might be experiencing the collective energy of a group, space, or planet, like the collective shock of a town recovering from a natural disaster or the collective stress of an open-area office on a tight deadline.

- You might be experiencing your own emotions that are coming up for processing.

The following exercise takes only a few minutes to help you get clear on whether the overwhelming emotion is yours or someone else's.

1. Find a quiet moment to tune in to yourself.

2. Put your hand over your heart to connect with and ground yourself. Take a few deep breaths.

3. Name what you're feeling: fear, anxiety, sadness, frustration, etc.

4. Now silently ask yourself "Is this emotion mine or someone else's?" Do you get images of bills piling up at home that are causing you stress? This indicates the emotion is yours. Or do you see a mental image of your spouse pacing the kitchen floor, venting about work stress that isn't a threat to their job or your family's stability? This would indicate the emotion mainly belongs to your spouse. Remember: The answer could also come to you as a voice in your mind (like hearing "Thailand" and realizing you're upset by a recent world event), as a mental download (like having a breakthrough thought that you're more worried about your teen than you realized and this emotion is yours as a concerned parent), or as a feeling (like thinking of a loved one who has been down lately and getting chills when you realize their depression may be affecting you in some way).

5. Take action. If it's your emotion, get support, let yourself feel it, lean in to your self-care, and discern what action step this emotion is asking you to take. If the emotion is someone else's, this does *not* mean you have to avoid that person or situation—it might mean, though, that you need to have better boundaries. If it's collective energy, take action by making a donation, saying a prayer, or doing anything else that's appropriate, peaceful, and helpful.

Sometimes just getting clear on how someone else's emotions are affecting you helps to keep you more grounded in your own energy.

> If you ever feel out of control with an emotion, get help. Ask for support from loved ones, colleagues, and healthcare professionals. Being an empath does *not* mean you need to suffer silently. Your tender heart is needed in the world, so take good care of yourself!

Tune In to Someone Else's Good Vibrations

Because empaths can easily absorb what's in their environment, if you're feeling bored, uninspired, or defeated, you can give yourself an energy boost by tuning in to the good vibes of others. It's like taking your soul for a scoop of ice cream! Pick someone or something to tune in to that won't be triggering. (If you've been trying to conceive for a few years and are frustrated, watching videos of cute newborns probably isn't best. Watch videos of dogs being silly instead.)

Here are some fun ideas for tuning in to good vibrations.

- Go to your favorite inspirational *Instagram* or *Facebook* account. (Find me @tanyacarrollrichardson or Facebook.com/TanyaRichardsonBlessings.)

- Call a friend who just fell in love, got a promotion or had anything else wonderful happen and let them gush.

- Put on a fun, upbeat song and dance around the house for 5 minutes (this works wonders).

- Visit a site that shares uplifting stories, like Ted.com, and hear about someone overcoming a big obstacle and finding success, peace, health, purpose, strength, forgiveness, or love.

- Watch a documentary about an underdog sports team winning a big championship or watch a clip of someone giving an emotional acceptance speech at an awards ceremony.

- Make a date to hang out with a loved one whose bubbly energy or positive attitude always uplifts you.

- Play with a child and see how often you can make them smile.

  Find good-vibe sources and piggyback on their positivity.

QUIZ: How Much Energy Do You Spend Tuning In to Others?

Tuning in to others automatically, as opposed to mindfully, or having a pattern of not anchoring in to your own energy is like having a tiny, undetectable puncture in a tire that causes the steady leak of air. Just like that tire, over time your energy will leak out and you will become drained and deflated.

Answer the first set of prompts with *often*, *sometimes*, or *rarely*. Answering *often* indicates you may be having trouble tuning out of others.

_____ I find myself trying to problem solve other people's issues in my mind.

_____ When I interact with a client or loved one who is very anxious, I'll often feel anxious after our interaction.

_____ When I see something upsetting on the news, it can be difficult for me to let go of it, even after I've processed my emotions, shared with someone, or taken an action step to try and help.

_____ When I'm concerned about a friend or loved one, or even a coworker I don't know well, my heart goes out to them. But it can be hard for me to disconnect from that concern and heart energy, which can leave me feeling vulnerable and raw for hours or even days.

_____ Being in a crowded or busy area, like a packed store, subway, or movie theater, can frazzle my nerves to the point that I'm completely unsettled after.

_____ When I'm taking care of others or very busy with work, I forget to eat, exercise, rest, get my hair cut, go to the doctor, and perform other basic self-care tasks.

Answer the second set of prompts with *often*, *sometimes*, or *rarely*. Answering *often* indicates you may be very good at mindfully tuning out of others.

_____ After I speak to someone who is upset, whether I know them casually or well, it usually doesn't take me long to move on to another task or take my mind to another subject.

_____ When someone is hurting, my heart may go out to them, but other times my witnessing energy kicks in instead. I feel genuine compassion for them, yet their pain does not significantly alter my inner emotional landscape.

_____ I like to stay informed regarding causes I care about—whether it's conserving natural resources, helping animals, or helping humans in need. As long as I practice balance, it *usually* doesn't over-whelm me emotionally, so I can be present, involved, and helpful.

_____ I find that when my self-care practice is dialed in, I have a much higher tolerance for situations that could potentially be draining.

_____ If a friend is draining because they have a habit of always treating me like their therapist, always dominating the conversation, and rarely showing concern for or interest in me, I will lovingly try to change the dynamic by turning the conversation toward me, talking to them compassionately about the unhealthy pattern, or limiting my time with this person.

_____ I'm pretty in touch with what issues I'm trying to work on in my life and what my long-term and short-term goals are.

Remember that there are no right or wrong answers; there is just self-reflection. Let your answers inspire you to take better care of yourself.

Deal with People Who Dump
Their Energy on You

We've all encountered "energy dumpers." It could be a manager who approaches your desk during big deadlines completely stressed out and scattered, or the loved one who lately seems to call only when they're so worked up they're screaming or hysterically sobbing. These are not bad or unkind people, and occasionally *you* might be considered an "energy dumper" by someone else! For an empath, being the recipient of an intense energy dump can feel toxic. Try this protocol.

1. Stay calm.

2. Enter observer mode by pulling back energetically and imagining space between your energy body and theirs. If you're on the phone, grab a heart-shaped stone or other grounding object and hold it.

3. Don't mirror their energy. If you replicate their emotions, drama increases. Resist the tendency to mirror energies and emotions.

4. Meet the other person with an even, grounded energy. Speak in a soothing or neutral way and keep your body language relaxed.

5. Notice if not mirroring their intense or very emotional energy defuses the situation. Your calm energy might alter the other person's. It's an empath Jedi mind trick!

6. Stay in witnessing energy if the other person is still dumping. Help or listen as long as that feels productive or healthy.

If this behavior is frequent, ask a counselor or other informed third party for advice. Remember that the person dumping on you could be really suffering or feeling out of control and need help. Move forward in a thoughtful and kind way as you protect yourself.

Work with Black Tourmaline

Some empaths are very sensitive to the healing, grounding energy of crystals and rocks. Black tourmaline has a protective quality that can be particularly beneficial for empaths, as this stone can help keep unwanted or draining energies at bay. Luckily, black tourmaline is inexpensive and you don't need a ton of it to reap its benefits. However, working with a larger piece might give you bigger results. You could:

- Wear it in jewelry, like a necklace, ring, or bracelet.

- Keep a smaller piece in your purse, backpack, or the fifth pocket of your jeans—what empath and spiritual teacher Tess Whitehurst refers to as the "crystal pocket"!

- Put a piece near the entry to your home, like in the pot of a plant.

- Place black tourmaline in a central common area of your home, where its energy can disseminate throughout your space, like on a mantel or kitchen countertop.

- Hold a piece of black tourmaline in your hand while you speak on the phone to someone who drains you or can be triggering.

- Keep this stone in your office if you're a healer.

- Store a piece in the glovebox of your vehicle.

- Keep a piece of black tourmaline near your bed if you've been experiencing bad dreams.

An empath friend who is extremely sensitive to energy—including the energies of wandering spirits or ghosts, which can sometimes inhabit spaces—finds black tourmaline so protective that he travels with a piece in his suitcase so he is never without it!

CHAPTER 4

Nurture Your Own Energy

Empaths may mistakenly feel responsible for other people's energies and emotions. First, because empaths can so intimately experience the energies and emotions of others, it's easy to then feel as if the next step is to try and help them. And sometimes helping *is* the right next step—but it is a step that should always be taken mindfully. Remember that as an empath you need to have especially strong boundaries. In this chapter, we'll cover empath-specific self-care techniques that help you maintain those boundaries when you're tempted to feel responsible for other people's energies and emotions.

The second reason empaths may feel responsible for or want to control the energies and emotions of others is a sort of self-defense or self-protection. Empaths might subconsciously think that if they can calm someone down or make them smile, then they won't have to feel any of this other person's challenging or intense energies or emotions secondhand.

That approach can work as a temporary fix, but in the long run only makes things worse for both parties involved. For empaths, it's vital to remember that you really can have power over only your own feelings. Even then, feelings are more often meant to be felt than controlled. Trying to manipulate, hold, or manage someone else's emotions takes you away from your center, from yourself, and from your power.

Empaths can be amazing sources of emotional support for loved ones, clients, coworkers, and anyone else they come in contact with.

Yet your unique empath ability to show up for others emotionally and energetically depends upon the balancing act of showing up for yourself first and staying mindfully grounded in your own energy. You do that primarily through your self-care practice.

Taking good care of yourself is priority number one and helps you be even more supportive to others. In this chapter, we'll go over mindful ways to nurture your own energy!

Align to the Energy of Grace

When beneficial people, opportunities, resources, or experiences show up for you right when you need them, that's grace in action. Grace is a mystical, supportive force that is always operating in your life. You can mindfully increase the number of moments of grace you experience and more fully activate this energy anytime you like. Whether you are facing a specific challenge or just want extra support, aligning to the energy of grace is an excellent way to take care of yourself.

Here are some methods for aligning to grace energy.

- Think of the world as a magical, loving place. Really difficult, painful things happen, but remind yourself that miracles happen too.

- Look on the bright side of situations, find the silver lining, and stay hopeful about the present and the future.

- Use a grace mantra, like "Unexpected blessings are always showing up for me."

- Anticipate mercy and second chances.

- Be kind to others as often as you can.

- Stay open to new experiences, people, and opportunities, and remain flexible.

- Speak honestly yet try to stay positive with your words.

As you align even more to grace energy, here are a few things to watch out for.

- Don't deny your own challenging emotions. You can be very sad or angry about something that's happened and still stay hopeful about the future or focus on the silver linings in the present.

- Be optimistic but also be realistic. Remain grounded about the facts of a situation.

- Take responsibility and take action where you can.

- Learn from the past, yet keep looking forward and remember that the future can be different and better.

I experienced grace in action many years ago when I was looking for an apartment in Manhattan. The initial two weeks of my search were very disheartening. I felt scared and defeated. However, I'd just gotten turned on to the power of positive thinking, so I thought "Well, let me try to switch my attitude and my expectations." I began thinking things like "I'm a good person and a good tenant, and anyone would be lucky to have me live in their building." My energy had been stressed, hurried, and closed off the past two weeks, so I purposefully relaxed, opened up, and slowed down. Within days I met a sweet real estate agent, and the first place she took me to was my dream apartment—in a brand-new building, in a sought-after neighborhood, with a beautiful park only blocks away. The price was astoundingly affordable. My husband and I lived there for thirteen years, and every time we walked through the front door we were reminded that miracles are real.

To align more mindfully with grace in your own life, take one situation that's been frustrating and change your attitude and your approach via the suggestions in this exercise. Notice if this changes your energy to one that's calmer and more hopeful, and watch for changes in the outer world too.

Allow Yourself to Feel Good Even When Others Don't

If a loved one, or the outside world, is going through a challenging time, it's all right if life still feels pretty good in your neck of the emotional and energetic woods. Remember that:

- You don't need anyone's permission to feel your positive feelings. Part of your self-care practice should be celebrating and savoring whatever is going well in your life.

- Taking on the challenging emotions of others won't help them. In fact, it will likely make things worse for both of you.

- Empaths are best at supporting others when they are taking great care of themselves. Taking on the energies and emotions of others is poor self-care.

When someone else is in a challenging place but you're not, try the following:

1. Practice focused support. Give someone your full attention when you are supporting them, then take your attention elsewhere.

2. Put time limits on your support. It's okay to notice the time when a friend is venting to you on the phone.

3. Find someone else to share your happiness with.

4. Compassionately and mindfully honor a loved one's—or the world's—pain. Step up your activism, make a donation, make someone dinner, or just tell someone you care.

Letting yourself feel wonderful experiences is how you stay balanced. Savoring and celebrating are good self-care!

Create an Intimacy Checklist

Empaths can bond with others very quickly because empaths can so easily sense how other people are feeling or what they need. Bonding easily with others is a useful and lovely ability, but it also has a challenging aspect—you can get too close too fast and end up hurt, realizing later that you did not yet know the person well enough or long enough to become so open and vulnerable.

Being intimate quickly isn't necessarily a bad thing. Sometimes a potential dear friend comes into your life out of the blue just when you need that sort of relationship most. This empath ability to get close quickly can also be quite valuable in certain work scenarios, like when you're new to a job but can quickly discern what a boss's temperament is like or how you can contribute to the existing team in a unique way. Yet empaths should be careful around this phenomenon.

Consult the following checklist when you're becoming intimate quickly with a new friend, extended family member, coworker, lover, or anyone else. You could also create a personalized checklist using some of the following questions while also coming up with your own.

- How does this person treat themselves? Do they seem to have a good sense of self-love and a healthy self-inventory process?

- What's the drama factor in our relationship? Have we already had intense fights or have I questioned the relationship already?

- How long have I known this person—days, weeks, or months?

- Does it feel like we have a soul connection or deeper bond?

- Do this person and I have any mutual friends or acquaintances?

- How much do I know about this person's past?

- Has this person been given the opportunity yet to show up for me in a significant way or have my back? If so, how did they do?

- Does this person try to make me responsible for their emotions?

- Does this person make me feel frazzled or drained, or does their presence make me feel more grounded and calm?

- Does this person give me my own space?

- Does this person genuinely care about my health and happiness?

- How does this person speak to me? Is it with kindness and respect?

- Am I in a relationship with this person because I sense they need me, or because I get something nourishing out of having them in my life?

- Is it difficult for me to set emotional boundaries with this person?

- Have I secretly wondered if this person may not be the best fit for me as a friend or lover or colleague at this particular point in our lives? *Or* does it seem like we met at the perfect time?

- Is this person generally supportive of my dreams and hopes?

- Is this person's natural energy a good fit for me, or does it feel a bit too intense or a bit too mild for me?

- Does this person seem flexible or open to change if something in our relationship isn't working?

Remember that the questions on this list aren't meant to judge you or the other person. The answers will simply help you get clear on the dynamics of your current relationship with them.

Practice Radical Self-Love

Empaths can be susceptible to internalizing the critical opinions of others about themselves. If someone is really angry at you or really disappointed in you, you may feel the other person's emotions strongly and intimately. If you're already in an emotionally heightened and vulnerable place, it can be more difficult to engage witnessing energy to get that eagle perspective of your higher self.

Radical self-love and self-acceptance are antidotes to being overly judgmental and harsh with yourself. Use the following self-love techniques for balance when you're in a challenging place with yourself, or use them anytime as effective self-care.

- When you catch a glimpse of yourself in the bathroom mirror at home, smile, wink, or look in your eyes and say "I love you!"

- Find a cute, happy picture of yourself as a child, frame it, and place it somewhere you'll see it often. Remind yourself that this lovable child is still part of you.

- If you're upset with yourself about the past, close your eyes and imagine yourself at the time of the difficult event. Silently send that younger version of you unconditional love and offer a quick, wise pep talk.

- If you've disappointed yourself or you regret an action, get your journal and write down five ways you have changed or want to change for the better because of this experience or five things you learned from it. Five is a number associated with positive major life changes.

- Serenade yourself by putting on a tender love song and singing it to yourself. Singing will open your throat chakra, which helps you express and process emotions.

Recognize Intense, Neutral, or Mild Energy

Having a classification system for different types of energies can help empaths be more aware of how the energies of others might affect them. Energy can have many subtle layers to it, and energy can be individual or collective. For instance, a national tragedy could create an atmospheric energy of grief, yet also have undercurrents of healing and connection. We might classify this energy as intense. Certain people or places might idle at different energies too, like a quiet town that is described as sleepy (mild energy) or a therapist who is grounded (neutral energy). Here's how each type of energy might affect you.

- **Intense energy** has the capacity to affect you in a big way. If a friend with a naturally intense energy is on top of the world, they can be a joy to be around as you open up to feel some of that sparkle! If the same friend is frustrated, you may want to engage witnessing energy to have good self-care boundaries.

- **Neutral energy** can be nourishing, like a blank canvas that allows empaths to tune in to themselves. You may find when there are no intense deadlines, and people are content in their positions, that your office has a comforting, neutral background energy.

- **Mild energy** can be a nice break—or it can become boring. Life is best with a balance of energies, and every empath will have different preferences and tolerances, at different times, for mild and intense energy.

Practice assessing energy as intense, neutral, or mild. People, places, and groups can have a baseline or natural energy and also experience drastic energy swings or subtle shifts. It's normal for people, empaths included, to be a fascinating, fabulous mix of different energies.

Detox from Gossip

For this exercise, you will try to avoid engaging in (which also means listening to) celebrity "news" and family or workplace gossip for two weeks. Diplomatically bow out of or redirect conversations that involve gossip without judging the person gossiping or creating unnecessary drama.

Both during this two-week period and afterward, whenever you find yourself attracted to stories about others, ask yourself:

1. **Does this information directly affect me?** If a coworker is gossiping about how your boss is switching departments, the answer may be yes. If the gossip is about the personal details of a manager's divorce settlement, the answer is probably no. That's the type of gossip you should avoid for the next two weeks.

2. **Does this information help me better connect to myself?** A friend might be sharing a story about their sibling, and how this sibling is going through so many big changes at once that it's causing them to feel ungrounded. If you are also struggling to stay centered while facing many big changes, this "gossip" could help you get more in touch with your own emotions, and listening to some of the details for a brief amount of time is fine for this exercise. If, however, you catch yourself reading about a celebrity's rehab stay just because you're bored at work, you should mindfully and lovingly find something else to occupy your mind over the next two weeks.

After this mindful gossip sabbatical, you will probably develop a different relationship with celebrity news, as well as family and workplace gossip, and be better able to discern when hearing or reading about others is healthy and when it is toxic, clogging up your sensitive system unnecessarily.

Release Someone with Love

When you care deeply about someone, it's normal to hold them close to your energetic heart. But when a relationship significantly changes or ends, or it becomes painful to hold someone close, it's healing to release them. This release happens on an energetic plane, and simply changes the level of intimacy between you and the other person. Because empaths are so sensitive to energy, lessening the energy connection between you and another can have amazing positive influences on you and even on the other person on the physical plane! Yet you don't have to let the other person know about this exercise or communicate with them—so it's a great option for a breakup or for creating mindful distance from someone who is still in your life.

The practice of releasing someone with love can help you do many healthy things, like:

- Process through painful emotions more easily or quickly.
- Forgive or accept the other person or find peace for yourself.
- Move on from a relationship and get closure.
- Bring new relationships into your life.
- Have a more neutral, and less triggering, experience when you interact with this person.

Try this ritual on any relationship. (If the other person makes you feel physically or emotionally unsafe, seek professional help.)

1. Create a healing atmosphere—play sacred music, light a candle, hold your favorite crystal, or burn some incense.

2. Imagine the energy around you becoming soft and loving. Picture the energy as pink, gold, or green, colors associated with the heart and healing. Take deep breaths as this energy washes over you.

3. Close your eyes and picture a healing sanctuary. It might look like a beautiful room with soft pillows to sit on and lovely sunlight streaming through the windows. Or it could be outside, like a field of wildflowers gently swaying in the breeze where you can lay a comfy blanket and sit. Your healing sanctuary might look very unique, like the tower chamber in a large castle lined with stunning tapestries. Take a moment and let your intuition and imagination fill in the details. You can visit this healing sanctuary anytime you like. If you have a spirit guide, loved one who has passed on, or angel you like to work with, call them in to be with you.

4. Picture yourself in your healing sanctuary. Next, think of the person you want to release. You might imagine writing their name on a piece of paper, or you might summon an image of their face. Send their soul the silent message that you wish them well and hope all the best for them. Tell them you are releasing them from their connection to you, and say anything else that feels right.

5. Notice (with your eyes still closed, resting in your healing sanctuary) what emotions come up in you. Let yourself feel them, and make a note to come back to them after you close the ritual.

6. Take in the details of your healing sanctuary one last time, and say goodbye to it for now. Slowly open your eyes. Take some deep breaths with your hand over your heart to close the ritual.

A lot of emotions or intuitive hits about next practical action steps might come up for you. Get support from loved ones or healthcare professionals, and know that releasing someone is a process that can't usually be completed with one ritual. As emotions come up around this issue in the following days or weeks, let them. When your mind returns to this person, think "I'm releasing them with love," and feel the gentle, peaceful energy of that intention in your heart.

Confront Others While Protecting Yourself

Empaths sometimes shy away from confrontations because they fear absorbing the challenging energies and emotions that confrontations can bring out in others. Yet sometimes confronting others, or openly disagreeing with them, is an important part of enacting change. Telling someone else how you really feel or what you really think helps you stay connected to yourself, honor your emotions, and practice self-care. It's also a way to honestly show up for other people to their benefit.

Try the following empath-friendly confrontation technique the next time you need to confront someone.

1. Process your emotions ahead of time. Share the raw ones with a trusted person, like a good friend or counselor.

2. Think through what you want to say and what you hope to accomplish in the confrontation beforehand.

3. Use your empath ability to tune in to what the other person's emotional experience *might* be. You could get the intuitive information that a romantic or business partner is scared about the future or overwhelmed with work and that's why they're being so rude to you lately. View any insights you get with healthy skepticism. After all, you may or may not be correct. This step is meant to help you see the other person more compassionately or holistically and remind you that other issues that have nothing to do with you might be at play.

4. Take a few minutes just before you confront this person to enter observer mode and engage witnessing energy. Get relaxed and grounded, perhaps by meditating, listening to nature sounds, telling yourself a supportive mantra, or picturing a ball of healing golden or blue light around your body.

5. Tell the other person how you feel and what you want as calmly and diplomatically as you can. Give them space to respond, and really listen.

6. After the conversation, pay attention to any new intuitive insights or emotions you experience about the situation.

While it may be naturally more challenging for empaths to confront others, it's a skill worth honing and an aspect of life worth making peace with, both for your personal and professional lives. If confronting others is tough for you, keep trying, get more support or tools, and practice radical self-love through the process.

QUIZ: Are You Acting As a Diplomat or Trying to Manage Other People's Emotions?

Empaths are often natural diplomats and negotiators because of their ability to tune in to others and understand where they are coming from. Empaths can also be good at communicating the perspective of someone else to a larger group—like to a family, a group of friends, or an office full of people. Yet empaths can confuse being a diplomat with needing to control someone else's emotional response—or talking someone else out of their emotion or truth if it is particularly challenging to others. Additionally, empaths might become admired among loved ones or colleagues for their negotiating skills and then be called upon to act in this capacity so often that it becomes draining.

Stay aware of whether you are operating in the healthy or unhealthy territory of your empath ability with this quiz. Answer *often*, *sometimes*, or *rarely* to the following set of prompts

_____ I'm always having to be the "bigger person" at home or work, and I feel like my emotions and needs are never expressed or honored.

_____ Many times it feels like the communities I'm part of are acting in ways that are less emotionally mature than me.

_____ There are people at home or work who can barely be in the same room unless I'm there to de-escalate things.

_____ If people at home or work are upset, I feel upset too until I can get them to calm down or feel better.

_____ Other people often ask "Can you talk to someone for me?"

_____ If I'm not at a work meeting or family gathering or other group activity, I fear someone may act out and I won't be there to help.

_____ I often find myself doing damage control for the words or actions of others.

If you answered *often* to many of the previous prompts, you may be trying to manage other people's energies or emotions, or acting as a shadow rescuer. Sometimes you might find that your attempt to manage the unhealthy actions or inconvenient emotions of others actually escalates matters—as well as drains you. Now answer *often*, *sometimes*, or *rarely* to the next set of prompts:

_____ Being the diplomat between people at home and work is one of my strengths: People recognize it, people respect me for it, and I honestly enjoy this role when I have the emotional reserves and physical energy.

_____ I feel comfortable telling two people that I don't have time to help them negotiate with each other if I'm drained.

_____ Sometimes I think it's best to let people make their own mistakes and learn their own lessons.

_____ Enabling people, or helping them stay in unhealthy patterns, is something I try to recognize and avoid.

_____ Even when I'm interpreting what someone else is feeling or wants to others, I make sure to express my own feelings and desires as well.

_____ Being treated with emotional maturity by others is important to me.

_____ When I need to take care of me, I stop and remind myself that I can't help others until I help myself first.

Did you answer *often* to many of these prompts? If so, you are probably in a good state of balance with your natural empath ability to be a negotiator or diplomat. If you find yourself being expected to constantly manage the energies and emotions of others at home or work, you might need to consciously change the energetic dynamic. Then you can—when it's a win for you as well as others—act as a healthy diplomat or negotiator, which can be a valuable and enjoyable skill!

Being more open to your own emotional experience by sharing and expressing it will actually help you be more open to the emotional experiences of others too. This can really improve relationships! Empaths don't have to repress their own emotions *or* try to contain the emotions of others.

Call On Archangel Chamuel for Peace

Empaths can have a special connection to spirit guides, who offer emotional and energetic support as well as bring people, resources, and opportunities into your life. Angels are loving, nondenominational beings who work with people from all cultures and faiths. Spirit guides existing in the energetic realm can be substantial allies for empaths, who are particularly open to energy.

Once an empath friend and I were hanging out at a coffee shop, chatting about self-care. "If you call on Chamuel," I explained to my friend, "that archangel will surround you like a soft, warm, fuzzy blanket and help your own energy feel more calm and content." I reminded my friend that when empaths call on a spirit helper, they might feel an energy shift in the room. At that moment, as we sat in a quiet corner of the coffee shop, an intense energy enveloped us both. It was strong, yet very peaceful and blissful. The energy cloud stayed for a few moments, and then began to lift. "What *was* that?" my friend asked, her eyes wide. "That was Chamuel!" I said. "Feeling is believing!" My friend got chills all over.

As you ask for this archangel's assistance—while you're commuting on the train, studying for an exam, or trying to stay centered during a crisis—imagine a soft, warm, fuzzy blanket surrounding you.

Angels and other spirit guides are never a substitute for competent human assistance—just a *complement* to it. If anxiety is an issue for you, get the help you deserve from healthcare professionals.

Say No with Love

Compassionate empaths, who may more easily fall into people-pleasing, feel empowered to say no when they can do so in a kind way. Try the following.

1. **Ask for space to think it over.** This allows you to go away and think things through as well as feel which answer is right for you without being influenced by the emotions of the person asking.

2. **Be careful with maybe.** If maybe really feels like the authentic answer, tell them that. Just don't use maybe only to soften the situation emotionally or buy time.

3. **Practice saying a firm no.** Once you're certain about your no, briefly role-play in your mind or with someone else. This gives you a chance to anticipate possible emotional reactions in the other person so you will be more grounded in the moment. A firm no is often kinder as it avoids drawing out uncomfortable emotions in you or others.

4. **Explain yourself.** Offer clear reasons for why you said no, assuring others that your no is not a reflection of how you feel about them. Saying an authentic no can be an act of grace for that person.

5. **Say yes in another way, if possible.** Since empaths are wired to feel other people's energies and emotions, if they can end the interaction on a positive or diplomatic note, it might simply be to their own benefit, provided the yes is authentic. This can also make your no more loving and generous. A dear friend might ask you to go on vacation to celebrate her milestone birthday, but the overseas location she suggests will be far outside your comfortable budget. You could offer to take a weekend trip together closer to home instead.

Build Your Escape Hatch from Crowds

You should not feel guilty about getting retreat-and-recover time during family reunion vacations, long work trips, or other situations where you may be around larger groups of people for extended periods. Taking nourishing time-outs isn't rude or selfish. It's simply a way to refresh and reset your energy.

Here are some creative ways to build your escape hatch.

- Say you want to take a nice long bath or shower after traveling. If you're mindful of your water usage, just sit in the bathroom and read or listen to a podcast!

- Explain that you're useless without your afternoon power nap. Then go to your room and meditate, journal, or actually nap.

- Tell others you have some work emails to catch up on, and after you quickly check them, take an extra 20 minutes to watch some funny or inspiring *YouTube* videos.

- Take your time getting ready to meet back up with the group. Put on some chill tunes, sing along, dance around, and slow your pace.

- Have a daily exercise routine? Grab your walking shoes or yoga mat and head out solo.

- Offer to dash out to run a quick errand for the group by yourself.

The more often you get healthy retreat-and-recover time in group situations, the more you will enjoy the people you're with—and they'll enjoy you more too, as your mood and energy will be improved! Remind yourself that enjoying the people you're with isn't about spending every second together like suction cups, which is very draining for empaths. Emphasize quality time over quantity time.

Summon Warrior Energy

Every empath has a strong warrior inside. You might summon this inner warrior to:

- Stand up for yourself or stand your ground with others.
- Speak your truth, no matter how it makes others feel.
- Anchor in to your own energy and perspective.
- Feel more confident, resourceful, and powerful in the world.
- Fight for the things that matter to you.
- Bounce back after a disappointment and be more resilient.
- Get through a challenging time.
- Rise to the occasion and shine.

Empath inner warriors are naturally fierce yet compassionate. Here's a quick method for summoning your warrior energy.

1. Use your imagination to get a mental image of this warrior. Does your inner warrior look like a character from a TV show, a historical figure, or someone in pop culture?

2. Give your inner warrior a mantra, like "I peacefully stand my ground," or "I'm stronger than I know," or "Watch me shine!"

3. Find a theme song for your inner warrior—choose something that makes you feel confident and powerful. You might hear this song as a synchronicity in a store or on the radio when warrior energy is required.

4. Move your body with gentle or moderate exercise, or watch videos of people performing amazing physical feats—like Olympic athletes competing.

Wise warriors never go it alone, so get support when you need it.

QUIZ: How Open Is Your Throat Chakra?

Chakras are energy centers located throughout the body, and the throat chakra—which helps you express yourself authentically—is located at the front of the neck near the hollow of the collarbone. Just like your physical body, your energy body is alive and always changing. You might go through a period when your throat chakra is very open and you feel safe and comfortable expressing your needs, desires, opinions, and emotions. At a different time in your life, those same expressions might be more difficult. The throat chakra is an important energy center for empaths to nurture so they can express emotions and advocate for themselves.

To determine if your throat chakra is open and healthy at the moment, answer *often*, *sometimes*, or *rarely* to these prompts.

_____ There are emotions I have now, or events from the past, that I avoid because they might be overwhelming.

_____ Nobody modeled healthy emotional expression for me growing up.

_____ Expressing myself might just cause drama and I may not get what I want anyway.

_____ I'm afraid if I tell people how I'm really feeling when I'm upset that the feeling will get worse or bigger.

_____ Even when I'm really happy or wanting to celebrate, I rein myself in.

_____ I won't share what I'm really thinking or feeling with others if it might change my relationship to them.

_____ I prefer to do a lot of my emotional processing internally.

If you answered *often* to many of these prompts, you might be going through a time in your life when expressing yourself has become more challenging. Now answer *often, sometimes,* or *rarely* to the next set of prompts.

_____ Right now I have people I can express myself to during tough times who are safe, healthy, and supportive.

_____ I like hearing or reading about the latest emotional healing and health theories and tools.

_____ Some days I'm better at advocating for myself than others, but it's generally a priority for me.

_____ I have people in my life who model healthy emotional expression.

_____ If I feel overwhelmed by an emotion or memories from the past, I know I need to get support.

_____ I have favorite ways and make space to celebrate wonderful times.

_____ I'm good at processing things internally, but I also value sharing as a processing tool.

If you answered *often* to many of these prompts, your throat chakra is probably healthy and open right now.

Working to heal your throat chakra is especially important for empath self-care and will help you savor all the good feels too!

Connect to Heart Wisdom

Empaths have a unique ability for connecting with the energetic heart, which has its own wisdom. I like to tell clients that the energetic heart contains the soul's memory. Heart wisdom is:

- Fair yet merciful.
- Honest yet compassionate.
- Aware that everyone and everything are interconnected.
- Tender, making you less judgmental and more forgiving or accepting of yourself and others.

Connecting to heart wisdom can give you special insight into a certain decision, situation, or person. Tap in to heart wisdom with these ideas.

1. Go away from a question for a bit and listen to music by a tenderhearted artist with heartfelt lyrics, or watch a movie where the characters show vulnerability and support each other.

2. Put your hand over your physical heart, take some deep breaths, and close your eyes. Feel the energy around your heart chakra grow, tingle, warm up, or activate. Now ask your heart what it has to say about this situation. Pay attention to any intuitive insights.

3. Connect with a loved one who is wise as well as kind and gentle. Tell them you're trying to come up with a heartfelt way to approach another person or issue and get their altruistic advice.

4. Think back to a time in the past when your heart was overflowing with love. Put yourself back there by recalling the details, especially those related to your physical senses. As the memory of that sweet energy vibrates through you, think about the decision you want to make and see if you get insights from a new, healing angle.

Create Energy Instead of Mirroring It

We've already discussed the concept of mirroring energy, which can be second nature for humans and easy for empaths. Yet empaths are also naturally gifted at, and can master the art of, creating energy!

Here's an example of how creating your own energy as opposed to mirroring another's can look. I once had a client (we'll call her Jane) whose partner was going through a rough patch in his career (we'll call him Mark). Mark was questioning his job and generally pretty moody. My client, Jane, had lots of exciting creative projects at work—outside of worrying about Mark, she was doing great. Mark and Jane carpooled to work downtown every morning to save money and the environment, yet mornings were when Mark's energy was most challenging. Jane, an empath, didn't want to abandon the carpooling, so she used the situation as an exercise in creating energy. As Mark would drive in brooding silence, Jane would listen to the happy songs on the radio, daydream as she watched the weather out the window, and concentrate on what she was looking forward to or grateful for that day. Sometimes Mark would even smile or engage pleasantly in conversation when he heard her singing along to the music or commenting about the gorgeous weather. Jane would stroll into work feeling good, and after several months Mark's situation and energy improved significantly. There were certainly days when Mark's mood still got under Jane's empath skin (especially if she was stressed or run-down). But knowing she could concentrate on creating energy instead of absorbing or mirroring it helped tremendously.

When creating energy, you're trying to nurture only your own energy, yet you might discover that others mirror your delicious energy back to you.

Address People-Pleasing, Rescuing, and Codependency Patterns

Part of a grounded empath's self-care practice is avoiding self-sabotaging patterns that empaths can fall prey to—like people-pleasing, rescuing, and codependency. What all these patterns have in common is not feeling okay until you make sure others are okay first.

While empaths might try to control their own inner emotional climate by managing the emotions of others and employing one of these patterns, this book is filled with many healthier ways to approach your emotions and those of others. Toxic coping skills, like codependency, take effort to heal—yet countless sensitive people have healed.

- *People-pleasing* is a tendency to do what you *think* is best for others with little regard to your own needs or desires.

- *Rescuing* is helping others who feel they are in desperate need in a way that can be unhealthy or even dangerous for the empath acting as life preserver. Some people—like EMTs—are rescuing in a healthy way.

- *Codependency* involves getting to a feeling of safety or worthiness through your relationship to someone else.

All of these patterns can enable self-sabotaging behaviors in others, so getting help is good not only for you but for others in your life too. If one or more of these patterns might be an issue for you, speak to a counselor about your specific situation. (There is simply too much to cover here.) Stick to information and helpful people who are knowledgeable, positive, and encouraging. These patterns do not change overnight, but with awareness and assistance they can heal dramatically over time.

Work with the Magic of Surrender

Surrendering an issue that feels beyond your control can be a powerful practice for empaths, because the energy of authentic surrender is light, peaceful, and positive—which can make energy-sensitive empaths feel the same way. The magic of surrender lies in its ability to let you step aside, make room, and invite the larger, benevolent forces of life to work on an issue for you, presenting you with new options. You might decide to surrender something because:

- You're frustrated with a situation and having trouble sticking with it.

- You don't know the best path forward after trying many options.

- You've become so emotional about the situation that some space or distance might help you think and act more clearly.

- You're a deeply spiritual person and you want a second opinion from the universe.

Surrendering is a change in attitude and energy. You still can and might have to keep taking action steps regarding this situation. The difference is that surrendering takes your focus off of trying to aggressively problem solve, control the outcome of, or make sense of an issue and allows your energy, mind, and emotions a restful pause.

For this ritual, gather a piece of paper and something to write with, a very small bowl or shallow teacup, a handful of rose petals (dried or fresh—if fresh, wait until the rose starts wilting and enjoy the flower as long as you can), and a small crystal or natural stone you like or feel connected to.

1. Write down on a small slip of paper, in a sentence or two, whom or what you're surrendering.

2. Take the paper and fold it up so it fits inside the bottom of your dish or cup.

3. Place the rose petals on top so they cover the paper. (You're using roses because they symbolize beauty, divine order, and balance.)

4. Gently lay your stone or crystal on top of the rose petals, like a mystical paperweight.

Leave your surrender offering somewhere you will notice it—on top of your dresser or by your car keys—for eight days. (Eight is a number of eternity and power.) Whenever you see or think of this tangible surrender offering, remind yourself you're letting the universe work on the situation while you take a step back. Watch for synchronicities from the universe as reminders that it's working on this issue. After eight days, you can throw away the paper or keep your surrender offering until the situation resolves or you feel more peaceful about it.

Observe Your Thoughts

An empath's thoughts can affect their energy, and while you don't want to restrict or police your thoughts—as they can give you important information about how you're feeling—mindfully observing your overly dramatic or negative thoughts is a healthy way to practice self-care.

When empaths get curious about anything—an interaction with a person, the outcome of a situation, or even their own thought patterns—they engage witnessing energy and enlist the eagle perspective of the higher self. There's no judgment or shame, just a little housecleaning in your head!

1. Get curious when a thought gets your attention as possibly overly dramatic or negative. For example, if you think "This will never work out for me" while you're looking at homes to buy, get curious about what's behind that thought and notice that you are feeling doubtful, frustrated, and tired.

2. Ask yourself: "Do I really *believe* this thought?" You might realize that you actually do believe you can buy a house, but it's going to take more time and effort than you anticipated. Shifts in approach and expectation are probably required.

3. Ask yourself: "Is this thought mine or someone else's?" It's very easy for an empath to take in what others are thinking and believing. You might realize that the thought started when you spoke to your mom months ago and she was pessimistic about the idea of you purchasing your first home. Or the thought might be one you picked up as a child because money was very tight for your parents and they never owned a home when you were growing up.

4. Revise your overly dramatic or negative thoughts to something honest yet kind and encouraging, like "It might be a difficult, long process at times, but I can buy a home I love." Think of this step as running your thought through your heart-wisdom filter.

5. Check in with your energy. Overly negative and dramatic thoughts have a heavy energy. See if working with this exercise makes your energy lighter.

Becoming aware of your thoughts and then examining and revising overly negative ones can truly change your energy, your attitude, your action steps, and even the outcome of a situation. While thoughts do *not* create your reality, they can positively influence the way you move through your life and the world.

CHAPTER 5

Work with the Energy of Spaces

Each space has its own unique energy. Empaths can quickly sense the energy of spaces, and you might walk into a space—like a yoga studio you're considering joining—and immediately feel at home, or you might walk into a store where you're applying for a job and feel that the energy doesn't mesh well with yours. In these examples, you'd also want to consider the classes a yoga studio offers or the rates a business pays its employees before making a choice. But empaths will put a lot of weight on the feelings they pick up about a space, which could be the deciding factor.

A friend and her partner were moving to a new town and had only one weekend to pick out a home! Their realtor had a dozen places to show them, and after they looked at the first house, my friend's partner said, "This is the one." My friend rolled her eyes. "We still have to look at the others." Her partner sighed. "Okay, but this is our house. It's just a feeling I have." Sure enough, eleven houses later, my friend admitted that her partner had been right. Yet it was also essential that this couple look at all their other options too. Trusting your empath instincts does not mean following them blindly.

In this chapter, we'll nurture the energy of any space you find yourself in. When a space has an energy that really resonates with you, it can have a huge positive impact on your own energy. We'll also explore techniques to improve the vibes in a space with challenging energy.

Create a Nature Nest

When you can't get outside to immerse yourself in nature's healing energy, try making a nature nest indoors. Your nest could live on a corner of your desk or in a nook in your bedroom, on the balcony of your apartment, or in the center of your kitchen table.

Create a small nature nest indoors and notice how this changes the vibes of the entire space. It might be made up of houseplants, fresh or dried flowers, natural stones, crystals, candles, incense, and/ or figurines (of spirit animals, for instance) that are meaningful to you. Small energy "power spots" that are curated in your home, office, or even a hotel room can have a positive, saturating effect on a space as well as on your energy.

Every day before I sit down to write, I create a nature nest beside my workstation that usually consists of fresh flowers or a small plant, one or two large crystals, a candle, and a few tiny angel figurines. You might consider bringing in an example from each of the four natural elements: fire, water, air, and earth.

Candles and incense are lovely "fire" energy enhancement tools, but always use them responsibly, never leave them unattended, and fully extinguish them when done. Share an image of your nature nest on social media with the hashtags #selfcareforempaths and #naturenest.

Call On Archangel Michael for Grounding and Protection

I refer to Archangel Michael as the hardest-working archangel in show business! This angel is certainly one of the most called upon and beloved spirit helpers, yet rest assured that Michael can work with countless people at once. That's partly because angels exist largely in the energetic, as opposed to physical, realm, and *arch*angels in particular have an enormous energy signature. Angels (who, like energy-sensitive humans, have a thinner emotional skin that absorbs a lot) love to support empaths like you. Archangels each have a unique energy and specialties. Archangel Michael's energy is grounding, formidable, and secure, and his specialties include protection, courage, faith, and strength. You might call on Michael to be with you in a space:

- When you're in a new space but have not yet gotten used to or warmed up the energy of this space.

- If you have trouble going to sleep at night in a certain space.

- If you want to feel more confident or powerful in a space, like at your office or at a venue where you will be performing.

- Whenever you want to create an energy buffer zone around yourself in crowded spaces, like large train or airport terminals. Think of Michael as an energy bodyguard!

- When you sense leftover energy from a past occupant of a space (or even a wandering spirit).

- When you find yourself in a space that makes you nervous or requires courage, like a hospital or courtroom.

You can perform this quick ritual anytime you need Archangel Michael's grounding, protective energy:

1. Quiet your mind and call on Archangel Michael. If you're at home, close your eyes. If you're in public, just think of this spirit helper's name. If you have an image of Michael, call that to mind too. You might also picture Michael as a blue-tinged ball of light or as a human who looks like you but with giant feather wings.

2. Notice if you feel an energy shift. Archangel Michael has a strong energy, so you might feel a significant shift. If the energy feels the same, don't fret—this angel always shows up and quickly.

3. Tell Archangel Michael in your thoughts what you need assistance with—like feeling comfortable in a new space, protecting your energy in a hectic crowd, or getting a good night's sleep.

4. Take a few deep breaths as this archangel's energy works its magic around you. Quickly picture Archangel Michael beside you (and you may feel an energy on one side of your body, like gentle pressure against your right arm), holding your hand, or lightly placing his hands on your shoulders (again, you could feel gentle pressure any of those places on your body). You can also picture Michael simply standing in the corner of a room guarding the energy around you.

5. Go about your activities normally. One important note: If you're genuinely feeling physically or emotionally unsafe in a space, enlist help from other humans ASAP.

As you try the exercises in this chapter, notice how you feel before and after. Stick with rituals that prove consistently beneficial to you, but periodically try new self-care practices—that will keep your energy curious, open, and flexible!

Pull Up Energy from the Earth to Feel Rooted and Stable

Sometimes our lives—and the physical spaces we inhabit—can be in a state of transition. A childhood home might be sold to someone outside the family; you could move to a new city and suddenly be in many unfamiliar spaces; or you might feel disconnected from the office and job you've worked at for years yet not know where the next office and job will be.

Change—including changes to familiar spaces or being in new physical spaces—can be disorienting and even a little scary. I remind clients that even really positive changes—like moving into your dream home—can be unsettling. Some part of the transition could even trigger a past trauma and make you feel extra vulnerable.

Pulling up stabilizing energy from the earth reminds empaths that they're already home, here on this planet, wherever they go. You can pull up energy from the earth to feel more rooted anytime, anywhere.

1. **Root chakra meditation:** Sit comfortably on the ground or floor, and imagine your root chakra, which is located at the base of your spine near the tailbone, as a cord of light that is stretching down into the earth. Picture the cord extending through any wood or concrete between you and the earth, even if you're in a building many stories high. Take some deep breaths and let the earth's energy come up and replenish your root chakra. You might feel more clearheaded, steady, or assured afterward.

2. **Rooting through the feet:** There are also powerful chakras on the bottom of your feet—just thinking of them might awaken these energy centers and cause physical sensations there. You can also gently massage the bottom of your feet to connect with these chakras. As you walk around or place your feet on the ground, no

matter where you are, remind yourself these chakras are connected to the earth's energy and drawing up that stabilizing force into your own system with every step, like drawing water from a well.

3. **Thanking the earth:** There's an exchange going on, so the earth was nourished by your energy as well. You can also thank the earth in a prayer or blessing, or by making a donation of time or money to an environmental charity.

Since the earth is our collective home, being good to the planet could be considered part of an empath's self-care routine. Identify the ways you're already living green and find a few new ways to up your game!

Rely On Healing Touch to Feel More Comfortable

Gentle, loving touch is a primal way to find comfort. Healing physical touch can help empaths feel more comfortable in physical spaces that might be energetically challenging, like:

- A hotel room you've never slept in before.
- A doctor's or dentist's office.
- An office where you're interviewing for a job.
- A room filled with people who might make you anxious, like a restaurant where you're meeting a partner's family for the first time.
- Spaces where the energy is intense, like a crowded outdoor concert.

The following are ways to create healing touch.

- Snuggling up with a pet, a partner, or your cozy bedding.
- Gently patting your leg with your hand, or just resting your hands on your legs if you're sitting down.
- Sitting cross-legged (like in yoga class) so you can tuck your feet underneath you or even hold your feet with your hands.
- Holding someone else's hand.
- Holding a small stone, spirit animal or angel figurine, or empath talisman in your hand.
- Getting a hug from someone else or giving yourself a hug.
- Lathering up with a soap or gentle scrub in the shower.
- Resting your hand on your tummy or giving it a gentle rub.
- Massaging lotion into your hands or feet.

Whenever a human interacts with another person, there's an energy exchange—for empaths this is doubly true. The same is true of the energy exchange between empaths and physical spaces. Use healing touch to warm up the energy of any space you're in.

Cultivate an Empath Sanctuary in Your Home

Having a place in your home designated for quality retreat-and-recover time might encourage you to seek out more healthy retreat-and-recover time. This sanctuary can even be an oasis to look forward to when you're not home, like being able to stay calmer during a busy afternoon deadline at work knowing your empath sanctuary is waiting.

Your sanctuary could be a place that's all your own, like a painting studio/shed in your backyard, or it could be a shared space, like a bathroom in a home that you share with others. With shared spaces, you can develop a quick protocol for transforming this space into a sanctuary. For instance, silently set the intention that this space is now designated for sanctuary time and add in any sanctuary elements you like—putting on soothing music or spraying aromatherapy.

Here are questions to consider when creating your sanctuary.

- Where in the home does my energy feel most peaceful, open, and inspired?
- Where and when is it easy for me to have privacy?
- Which creative hobbies and intellectual or spiritual pursuits might I enjoy in my sanctuary?
- What sounds do I want to hear in my sanctuary?
- What energy or mood do I want to cultivate in my sanctuary?
- Is there a smell I'd like to experience in my sanctuary?
- Will there be any rules for myself or others about this sanctuary?
- How will I unwind in my sanctuary?
- Which healing, sacred, or special objects might I keep in my sanctuary?
- How will I decorate my sanctuary or will there be a visual theme?
- How can I make this space physically comfortable?

Cultivate an empath sanctuary that's a true place of refuge!

Shield with Bracelets in Public Spaces

Empaths are sensitive to both beauty and healing touch, so wearing attractive bracelets that feel good against your skin might be something you already do! But did you know that these bracelets can also act as an energy shield? Energy can travel up your arms, so having a bracelet or even a string on each wrist can be a way to minimize absorbing unwanted energy (and therefore banking or conserving your own). Some empaths believe the left is the receiving side of the body, and focus on that area. (I personally find it helpful to wear bracelets on both wrists.)

Bracelets can be a useful shielding tool when you're at a busy restaurant, you're attending a large conference, or anytime you're in a space with a lot of hustle and bustle. It's simply important that you find the look of your bracelets pleasing and the feel of them on your wrists comfortable. Some empaths prefer bracelets of small beads made from natural stones and crystals, which can help you feel *even more* grounded when you wear them. Here are some crystals and stones that empaths might enjoy wearing.

- **Rose quartz:** Connects to love, peace, and heart energy.
- **Clear quartz:** Encourages witnessing energy.
- **Jasper:** Promotes healing, earthly grounding, and balance.
- **Jade:** Attracts luck, grace, and blessings—like empaths, jade is both beautiful and strong.
- **Moonstone:** Enables mystical power, dreams, manifestation, and the imagination.
- **Amethyst:** Embodies awakening energy and intuition.
- **Amber:** Symbolizes power, ancient wisdom, and soul growth.

Try wearing any type of bracelets the next time you're in a large or hectic space and notice if you feel more grounded and calm.

Observe Empath Boundaries in the Digital Age

The digital universe—which includes the Internet, social media, and your phone—can be considered a specific space, and empaths always feel more comfortable when they develop ground(ing) rules around navigating unique spaces. Being more connected to others in the digital era has been a blessing for empaths, allowing them to find other empaths all over the world with whom they can share information about the empath experience. Yet it's important to be mindful of your empath sensitivity while you interact with digital offerings and platforms. In particular, you should:

- **Notice if the sites or feeds you go to regularly are nourishing and connecting.** While you want to stay informed about troubling events happening in the world (I read the big headlines as well as a few breaking stories every day, for instance), avoid overexposing yourself to traumatic news stories or celebrity gossip. All sites and feeds have their own unique energy and can encourage certain energies in you. Some empath-friendly sites and social media feeds you may enjoy include MindBodyGreen.com, OprahMag.com, SuperSoul.tv, PsychologyToday.com, Goop.com, MagicMondayPodcast.com, LightWatkins.com, LeeHarrisEnergy.com, CherylRichardson.com, RedTableTalk.com, ColetteBaronReid.com, RadleighValentine .com, SoniaChoquette.net, DebraSilvermanAstrology.com, GoddessProvisions.com, and AstroStyle.com. Most of these sites offer empath-friendly, free content regularly on social media or via email.

- **Practice the empath golden rule of balance with all digital offerings.** Set loose time limits around checking social media and surfing online, and stay present to actual 3-D people in your presence (like looking up from your phone when someone comes in the room), your own emotional experience, and offline life in general.

- **Try putting your phone in your bag or pocket.** That way, you're less likely to immediately look at it during every down moment, whether you're hanging out face-to-face with friends and family or by yourself. Resist the urge to check your phone when waiting in line, when waiting for someone else to arrive, or during other down moments. Instead, connect with your energy, notice your surroundings, or meditate. Downtime is a great time to invite in deep thoughts from your intuition and guides!

- **Talk about upsetting or triggering things you see online, as well as the joyful stuff.** If something online creates a strong emotional reaction in you, find someone you can share or unpack this with. Empaths love connection and sharing! The web is a tool to help humans stay more connected—not become more isolated.

- **Use social media to stay connected to other empaths.** The topic of sensitivity is becoming more popular and accepted. It's an exciting time when you can find many everyday empaths and experts sharing online. Check out what Dr. Judith Orloff shares on social media about the empath experience.

- **Maintain healthy emotional boundaries online as you do offline.** If your energetic heart goes out to someone you read about online, remember to come back home to your own energy afterward. If your head and heart are full of people online because they're funny, comforting, or fascinating, that's normal and healthy—just watch out for getting lost in the lives of others because, as an empath, you can so easily tune in to their experiences and emotions. Don't compare and despair. Come home to your life and emotional experience—it's safe and rich.

Just like any physical space, digital spaces deserve your mindful attention to be sure they are nourishing instead of draining your energy.

Nourish Your Adrenal Glands

Your adrenals help you regulate and manage stress, and part of maintaining a healthy, calm nervous system is nourishing these small yet very important glands of your endocrine system. Why does this exercise appear in the section about working with the energy of spaces? Nourishing your adrenals will help you better manage stress, and many empaths I've spoken with find that large spaces with lots of people or being in spaces of any size that have challenging energy are stress triggers.

Supporting your adrenals daily helps you manage the average stresses of life, but it's also like making a deposit in the bank every day. When you need your adrenals to manage higher-than-normal stress levels, they will be able to pull from those nourishing daily deposits—just like you would be able to pull from a bank account during a financial challenge.

Nourishing your adrenals might look like:

- **Avoiding unnecessary stress—especially in your own mind.** Sometimes, your own dramatic, worrying, or worst-case-scenario thoughts are a significant source of unnecessary stress, which can be very emotionally draining and even physically exhausting.

- **Developing healthy sleep patterns.** Go to bed and wake up at roughly the same times every day. When you have a regular routine, it helps your body better regulate hormone balance and manage stress.

- **Eating small meals throughout the day.** This tactic helps regulate your blood sugar, which can lower stress levels. Make sure you're getting enough protein, and speak to a doctor or other healthcare professional for specific dietary advice tailored to you.

- **Getting the nutrients you need to support your adrenals.** You might want to boost your intake of certain vitamins and minerals, like vitamin C and magnesium (you can buy gentle or buffered supplement forms of these nutrients). Always check with a healthcare professional—like a naturopath, nutritionist, or nurse practitioner—before taking a new supplement. Some nutrients that might be recommended for adrenal health, like sea salt, might be contraindicated for certain individuals.

- **Practicing moderation.** Avoid any extremes, like over-exercising, over-caffeinating, or even emotional extremes. Emphasize gentle activities and try to keep work and life in sensible balance.

If you're curious about adrenal health, or feel it might be an issue for you, don't guess at supplements and medications or self-diagnose. Find a knowledgeable, caring healthcare practitioner to work with!

Create an Altar in Your Home

Empaths might enjoy having small energy power spots, like altars, located throughout their homes. Unlike your empath sanctuary, which may encompass a whole room—like a small study or living room—your altar will usually occupy just a corner of a room, like a mantel. While your empath sanctuary might be transformed from a common area, like a bathroom, and then transitioned back to a common area, your altar is stationary. Your altar isn't just a place to retreat and recover; it's a place to connect with the sacred. Every empath's spirituality will be unique. Whether you are dedicated to one spiritual path or like to take what resonates with you from many different spiritual traditions, your altar might become an energy portal where you feel more connected to the Divine.

You might use your altar to:

- Perform a ritual.
- Meditate.
- Surrender something.
- Pray or say a blessing.
- Connect with your spirituality.
- Ask for guidance or support from Spirit.
- Store or work with divination tools.

Here's how to make your altar.

1. Designate a spot at home for your altar, somewhere you'll notice it but it won't be disturbed.

2. Decorate your altar with objects that have spiritual meaning for you, like a small statue of Buddha or Mother Mary, rosary or mala beads, tarot cards, runes, a photo of a guru, sacred books, a singing

bowl, a dream catcher, a Celtic cross, quotes from spiritual texts, or nature elements like pine cones.

3. Bless your altar. After setting it up, perform a little blessing ritual over your altar in whatever way resonates for you.

4. Keep the energy of your altar uplifting and engaging by periodically changing up the objects there, cleaning the altar, or just spending time holding or looking at the sacred objects there.

Developing a connection to Spirit—or the energy force that is larger than all of us, separate from all of us, yet part of each of us—can be a very meaningful and profound journey for energy-sensitive empaths.

Infuse a Space with Playful Energy

Playful energy takes the edge off life, and energy-sensitive empaths who easily pick up on everything—including life's edgier edges—can require regular doses of playful energy!

The following are methods for infusing a space—like a home, office, backyard, or classroom—with playful energy.

- **Make jokes!** Stick to jokes that are good-spirited and heart-centered. You can tease people in a playful *and* loving way.

- **Be kind and considerate.** When people treat each other warmly, it makes them and the energy of a whole space more relaxed—and naturally more playful.

- **Smile.** On some deep level, smiling at someone is a way of saying "We're all connected," and can make people feel safer. When people feel a sense of community, they are more likely to be playful.

- **Act silly.** Kids are wonderful at this, and I know many playful adults who also like to break into song or make funny faces.

- **Be mischievous.** Play a small, safe prank on someone. Give people unexpected gifts—or gag gifts.

- **Be zany.** Have zany yet appropriate objects in the space, like a funny sign, or dress in an appropriate yet zany way—over-the-top jewelry at work or pajamas with a zany print at home.

- **Get to know people well.** When you know someone well, you understand their sense of humor and it's easier to joke and tease. Laughter can also create more intimacy.

Practice infusing a space with playful energy this week—it's healing for your mind, body, and spirit!

Keep Spaces Tidy, Clean, and Uncluttered

Empaths should get clear on their emotional and energetic relationship to clutter, which can be different for each empath. An empath I knew who worked in a large open-area office with many other employees and stacks of papers, books, and other objects on nearly every surface told me, "There's a pretty furniture store across the street from my office with high ceilings and lovely plants and candles. Sometimes on my break I'll go sit there on one of the couches and decompress." A different empath might be unaware that they use clutter on their desk as a sort of energy shield, and need to find a better shielding method.

Many empaths are annoyed, distracted, and unnerved by clutter. Keep your space—and your energy—tidy, clean, and uncluttered with these tips.

- Declutter. As you examine your belongings, try the popular Marie Kondo method of asking, "Does this item spark joy?" If you're not sure, give yourself more time to consider before you start throwing things away or donating them.

- Be present with yourself emotionally as you declutter. Some clutter could be making you feel safer emotionally or acting as an energy shield; clutter might bring up strong or sentimental memories.

- Tackle the more obvious culprits first. While the stuff tucked away in "junk drawers" or closets is draining, the clutter you can see out all the time is even more draining.

- Organize the items left with shelving, colorful baskets, or neat-looking boxes.

Pick one manageable spot to start decluttering, so the process is less overwhelming. Pace yourself!

Decorate with Intention

Physical objects create certain energies and emotions in humans, like the painting you love that hangs in your hallway or the rug you hate in your father's living room. Empaths, who are hyper-perceptive and notice a lot about physical spaces, will want to decorate their spaces with colors, objects, artworks, and furniture pieces that create positive energies and emotions in them. A space you find intensely aesthetically displeasing can drain your energy. Many empath clients tell me there's a space in their home or office they've been meaning to beautify, but they can't find the time or energy. Then this space becomes even more of an energy drain.

Which space in your life needs an empath makeover the most? Take manageable, affordable steps to decorate with intention. Some things to keep in mind are:

- Less is more, since empaths can typically be bothered by clutter (unless they are unconsciously using it as an unhealthy energy shield). You don't need to spend money on a lot of stuff.

- Make the space your own authentic style—updating periodically as your style changes—so spending time in this space will be a way to re-ground and connect back with your own energy.

- When decorating, different colors, fabrics, designs, and objects can change your energy and affect your mood. Give a space the vibes test—does it promote good vibes?

Some empaths sense old energies around objects, perhaps from spaces they've previously inhabited. Clear the energy of an object by saying a blessing over it, placing the object in a bowl of flower petals, leaving it in the sunlight (be careful not to cause damage) or moonlight, smudging it with sage smoke, or simply giving it a gentle clean.

Create Cozy Energy

You might want to create cozy energy in a space because:

- You're physically tired or healing.
- You're going through changes or transitions and feeling vulnerable.
- You're upset emotionally and you want to calm down.
- You're with other people and want to create an atmosphere that encourages relaxation and emotional intimacy.

Create more nourishing, cozy energy by:

- Making a large space feel smaller. If you have a large backyard, create cozy energy in one corner of the porch.

- Having everything you need close by so you can snuggle into your environment, like keeping a book, your reading glasses, and your tea on a side table.

- Encouraging an atmosphere of plenty and generosity. If you're hosting others, offer fun snacks and drinks—anticipate what your guests would like so they feel nurtured, like putting out special options for people with food sensitivities or folks who do not consume alcohol.

- Creating physical comfort with pillows and throws. Keep soft blankets of different weights for different seasons, and lay a blanket over your body (some empaths love weighted blankets), pile petite pillows in your lap, or have oversized pillows arranged on either side of you. Feeling physically snug can calm sensitive people.

Many empaths might find cozy energy an ideal go-to for any mood. When you're with others, cozy energy can provide a lovely balance for empaths, where they are not feeling under- *or* overstimulated.

Clear the Energy of a Space

Spaces, like people, hold energy at all times. If the space you're in feels stressful, stagnant, or energetically cold and uninviting, you might want to perform a ritual to clear its energy. Clearing the energy of a space can also be done:

- As part of your regular maintenance of a space, like a home or office, after you physically clean it.

- Because the space is new to you and you want to clear any old energy from previous occupants.

- Because something just feels off or funky in the space energetically.

- Because there have been a lot of intense emotions flying around the space recently, like celebrations, work- or school-related intensity, or fights.

- As part of your own practice of grounding in to your energy.

Clearing the energy of a space can *clearly* be very useful, but it isn't recommended in certain situations. For example, don't try to use energy clearing to:

- Get rid of a wandering spirit. I've had clients tell me they tried to use sage to clear a strange energy they thought was a ghost out of their home, and this can actually exacerbate the situation. These energies need to be guided on to a better, healing, loving place. For more on this topic, see my book *Angel Intuition*.

- Avoid facing or dealing with a larger issue. If you're fighting with roommates or family members you live in a space with, energy clearing can definitely help sweep away that old energy and bring in more uplifting, fresh energy. But it won't magically solve the deeper issues going on. This ritual can, however, provide you time to connect with yourself to tune in to your intuition about what's really happening in these relationships and next best steps.

You'll need to choose a cleansing tool for this energy-clearing ritual: smoke (from incense in a small bowl, a stick of sage, or incense in a wand form), water (I like to use an aromatherapy spray), or sound (from a bell, tuning fork, rattle, or singing bowl).

1. Find a time when you can be alone in the space for 20 minutes to an hour or so (depending on the size of the space), and do a light physical clean of the space beforehand. Pick an instrument of smoke, water, or sound to use as your clearing tool. If you suspect that smoke or smells may bother you or anyone else who uses the space, stick to the sound or water tools. All are effective!

2. Get grounded before the ritual. Sit down in the space and enter a meditative state. Decide what energy you want to bring into the space and find a word for that energy, like *love, healing, peace, inspiration, forgiveness, kindness, mercy,* or *grace.*

3. Take your energy-clearing tool and slowly move around the space. If you're working with smoke, wave the incense stick or wand, or hold the bowl so the smoke moves around and fills the space. If you're working with sound, engage your singing bowl, strike your tuning fork, shake your rattle, or ring your bell and let the vibrating sound resonate. If you're working with water, spray your aroma therapy into the air and let the mist float. Gently focus on the energy you want to create that you already named—feel that in your body, speak that word aloud, or silently concentrate on a mantra, like "Peaceful, loving energy resides here."

4. Notice where the energy feels heavier or thicker. If you're in a home office, the energy around your desk might feel heavier because you've been working long hours or stressing about a project. If you've just hosted a big party and everyone was congregating in the kitchen, you might notice the energy is denser there. Spend more time on these areas until the energy feels lighter. Clear the corners of each room, where the energy can get stuck, and the center of bigger rooms, where the energy can radiate out.

5. Make sure to fully extinguish any instruments of smoke, and close the ritual in your thoughts or aloud with a prayer or blessing.

CHAPTER 6

Create Balance and Harmony

Balance is a central theme for grounded empaths. When your sensitive emotional and energetic systems feel well-balanced, life as an empath can be a very enjoyable experience! You shouldn't expect to be in perfect balance all the time, though—in fact, there's no *perfect* anything. When you feel out of balance, think back on a time—it could be two days ago or two years ago—when you felt really balanced. Use that feeling, and maybe the self-care techniques you were emphasizing then, as a guidepost that brings you back to balance. Some days, balance is less about hitting the bull's-eye and more about just getting your dart to land anywhere on the board. Part of your self-care routine will be harmoniously integrating your empath nature into the other aspects of yourself and your life, as well as trying to more harmoniously interact with the larger world.

With all the blessings of modern existence come more ways for your energy to become scattered, distracted, and drained. Yet the more you understand the principles and work with exercises in this chapter, the more you'll get clear on what a balanced life looks and feels like for you as an individual. For empaths, balance is your true home—it's created inside of you and you can take it with you anywhere.

Creating communities of other empaths—whether online, in person, or through a book like this one—helps normalize the empath experience but also allows empaths to share resources. If you notice another empath struggling with balance and harmony, offer some wise words or tools that have worked well for you.

Write Your Empath Heart a Love Letter

Increasing your self-love, especially around your empath ability, will help you better protect, advocate for, and celebrate this special part of yourself. I've long believed that self-love is a magical energetic X factor that can create miracles in your life. Remember to be gentle and kind with yourself as you write your love letter. This exercise can increase balance and harmony within if you've been having difficulty accepting or integrating something about your empath nature, you're just getting in touch with your empath nature for the first time, your empath sensitivity has recently experienced a growth spurt that you are still getting used to (simply working with the exercises in this book should help), or you've been dealing with more challenging/shadow aspects of your ability lately (like picking up on intense world energy or feeling overstimulated by the energy of others at work or home). Here are some writing prompts to get you started.

- This is something I absolutely love about my empath nature:

- In these ways, being an empath really suits my life, personality, family, or profession:

- In other ways, being an empath has been a challenge in my life or difficult for me. I've grown and improved around these issues, though. For instance:

- I'm getting clearer about myself and my empath nature in the following ways:

- I feel powerful as an empath when I:

- I'm proud of the following ways my empath nature has supported others:

- I'm grateful for the ways my empath nature has supported me, like:

- If there was something encouraging my higher self could say to my empath heart, it would be:

- In the following ways I have been brave about my empath experience:

- Some things about my empath nature I'm still learning to love or just accept include:

- My empath heart is resilient in the following ways:

- My empath heart is compassionate in the following ways:

- My empath heart is wise in the following ways:

- My empath heart is hopeful about the following things in my life and in the larger world:

Keep your love letter someplace special, like in your journal or tucked away where you keep your oracle cards, crystals, or other sacred objects. It might become a loving time capsule or message in a bottle to your future self!

Sensitivity is not static, and could increase at any time to help you navigate a challenging situation or because your sensitivity is increasing overall. Lean in to your self-care during sensitivity growth spurts, remembering that, in time, your heightened sensitivity will feel normal, just like when you went through a physical growth spurt as a child.

Use Creative Expression for Retreat-and-Recover Time

All empaths can benefit from having a creative outlet, even if you've never felt particularly artistic—you just might surprise yourself! Creative hobbies can be low-stress, and not only soothing but also energizing. Solo creative pursuits, like the following, are ideal activities for empath retreat-and-recover time.

- Writing, journaling
- Drawing, painting
- Knitting, sewing
- Photography, design
- Learning a musical instrument, songwriting
- Cooking, baking
- Sculpting, pottery
- Jewelry-making, woodworking

I knew a father (and empath) with several small children who was the primary caregiver during the day while his partner worked outside the home. Once his children were in bed at night, he'd go to his desk and work on a novel. Some nights he'd write for 3 or 4 hours. Other nights he wouldn't write at all. But just knowing his creative project was there, like a self-care bookmark, kept his overall life more balanced. People marveled that he could write a novel with his busy schedule, but that time spent writing (his version of retreat and recovery) was a key part of his empath self-care routine.

Is there a creative pursuit that makes you feel like time flies by because you're so engaged, relaxed, and happy? Can you find at least 1 or 2 hours a week to devote to this hobby?

Schedule a Gratitude Day

All empaths encounter challenging times once in a while, and these times can throw your energetic balance out of whack. For instance, you might have found out that you lost a job you love, you owe a ton of money in taxes, your partner wants a separation, or a dear friend is moving far away. Working with gratitude can make you feel a little less scared, angry, or sad during the more difficult seasons of your life. That's because gratitude itself has a lovely balancing quality to it. The energy of gratitude could be described in words as *humbling, content, thankful, blessed, present,* or *even-keeled.* Even if you scored one of the biggest wins of your life, injecting your celebrations with heartfelt gratitude will immediately bring your intense energy into a more neutral, peaceful place. When empaths are experiencing intense emotions, gratitude can bring emotional balance to your system if the intensity is becoming overwhelming.

1. Pick your gratitude day on the calendar. Give yourself a few days, a week, or even a few weeks to absorb the initial shock and process some of your emotions if you're experiencing something intense, then circle a day on the calendar in the near future with a big heart. Give yourself something to look forward to.

2. Figure out what you can do on the gratitude day to encourage feeling thankful. It might be taking yourself out to lunch at your favorite café, getting a spa treatment, having a romantic dinner at home with your partner, taking a day trip with a friend, visiting your favorite park or bookstore or museum, or doing anything else that typically makes you feel glad to be alive.

3. The evening before your gratitude day begins, let people around you know what you're up to. If you live with children, a partner, or a roommate, let them know tomorrow will be a day when you're

focusing on gratitude. Have a coworker who is also a friend? Let them know too. Tell pets what's up! Somehow they really will understand. Getting a few others on board can increase the good vibes, especially for sensitive empaths who are so in tune with the energy around them.

4. Think of something basic that you're grateful for when you wake up. Upon waking, you might be hit by a bunch of worrisome thoughts or heavy emotions about the challenging situation you're in (or if something really big and really good happened, you might wake up feeling intense and ungrounded). Just remind yourself that today is a bit of a break, and gently turn your mind to something small and manageable you're grateful for. You might be grateful to wake up in clean, soft sheets, grateful to wake up next to a snuggling person or pet, or grateful for that morning juice or tea.

5. Keep this pattern going throughout the day. When the worry thoughts and heavy or intense emotions come, don't try to fight them or stuff them down. Just remind yourself you're giving your energy a refresh day, like rebooting a computer, and gently find something small in the moment to be grateful for and focus on. Emphasize gratitude in your conversations with others. Focusing on how you're blessed today will help train your brain to look for more reasons to be grateful every day.

If you enjoy this exercise, you might try scheduling a gratitude afternoon one day a week, or a whole gratitude day regularly each month. While you face difficult situations and process through painful emotions—or even while you try to find stability and peace during big, positive changes—gratitude is a great way for empaths to keep their energy balanced. I believe this balanced energy that gratitude naturally invokes is partly why gratitude has become such a popular practice!

Work Effectively with Healthcare Professionals

Some empaths may find that their psychic sensitivity comes in the package of a sensitive physical body. Finding healthcare professionals to work with is an important part of staying balanced as an empath. You might need to find a counselor to enhance your emotional and mental health; ask a naturopath or nurse practitioner about your vitamin and mineral levels, hormones, or thyroid function; or work with a specialist physician to help you manage a chronic condition. Empaths might also like to partner with massage therapists or energy healers.

The following is a checklist for empaths to look over when considering their health.

- **Don't go it alone.** Experts are there for a reason. If you're scared to face a health concern or you have anxiety about doctors in general (like getting panicky when seeing the dentist), talk to a loved one or get support so you can give yourself the gift of better health. Sometimes sensitive people suffer from anticipatory stress, so the anxiety leading up to an appointment, procedure, or test can be the worst part for empaths. Refer to other ideas in this book to help you de-stress beforehand.

- **Remember that a caring bedside manner can be a big plus for empaths.** Because empaths are so sensitive to the energies and emotions of others and their surroundings, details like what a doctor's office looks like or how warmly they greet you when you arrive can mean a lot. Still, it's just as important to work with experienced people who can help you and get results. Sometimes a brilliant, dedicated doctor could come off as cold yet be the perfect person to partner with, so assess healthcare providers holistically.

- **Don't assume it's just your energy that's off.** Empaths could chalk up a period of sadness or exhaustion to challenging energy at the office or home, for example, or think they just need an energy clearing, when they really may be suffering from a physical imbalance like a mineral or hormone deficiency. Healthcare professionals can help you rule things out and get an accurate picture of all the factors affecting you.

- **Prioritize *your* health.** Empaths can be very compassionate and find themselves in the role of caregiver to others. While these caregiving roles can be very nourishing and fulfilling, watch out for burnout. Make sure you're taking care of yourself as well, and not downplaying your own health needs and concerns to your loved ones, clients and coworkers, or to your healthcare professionals.

- **Get more emotional support.** Whether it's letting a good friend know you need more support, or getting support from a trusted counselor or other healthcare professional, let people know when you're stressed, hurting, or emotionally drained. Find people who are good at staying grounded and being supportive when you need help. This will minimize an empath's fears of opening up and then having to feel all the difficult emotions their reveal could create in others. This is why counselors or coaches can sometimes help in ways loved ones will struggle to.

Whatever type of healthcare professional you're looking for, find the care you need and deserve!

Channel Someone Else's Energy for Inspiration

Empaths have a unique ability to feel someone else's experience intimately, and you can use this to your advantage to inspire yourself. If you're an entrepreneur, you might channel Oprah Winfrey's energy (confident, relaxed, expansive, and authentic). Need to psych yourself up for a big challenge that involves a long-haul commitment? Watch videos of athletes training or read about the construction of a historic landmark. Want to push yourself to perform even better than you have in the past? Listen to one of your favorite musical artists nail a live concert, or even watch an amateur singer or dancer nail a televised competition. As an empath, you can allow part of this person's healthy, inspirational energy to alchemize with your own. Here's how.

1. **Pick a person whose energy is inspirational and relatable.** Pick someone you not only admire as an artist, for example, but also as a human (like an artist who supports a charity you love). Or pick a neighbor whose parenting skills you admire.

2. **Immerse yourself in their energy.** Read interviews with this person or read their biography. If it's a friend who is a master at acceptance and taking disappointments in stride, set up a time to hang. If you want to channel your grandmother's energy of strength and resiliency, put a picture of her out where you can see it every day.

3. **Let yourself "try on" their energy.** If you're recovering from an injury or illness, remind yourself of someone in the news or in your life who healed from or learned to manage something similar. This could inspire your action steps.

Rebalance with this exercise anytime you notice your inspiration tank is a little low.

Prioritize Gut Health

Gut health plays a large role in your overall health. Having good digestion and a balance of friendly flora in your system can even positively affect your emotional balance—a priority for sensitive empaths. I personally spent many years managing a chronic illness and finally healed my own gut, so I understand how complex and unique each body is. I've seen the dramatic effect that gut health can have on energy levels, mood, and overall health—it's worth the time and effort to improve or maintain yours.

Here are some general gut-friendly tips.

- Watch out for unnecessary sugar in your diet or practice moderation. Remember that sugar doesn't just come from desserts, but also from wine, high-glycemic carbs, and fruit.

- Eat mindfully. Make time to prepare healthy meals and get to the store for healthy snacks/ingredients. Slow down when you eat and chew your food.

- Notice how your body responds to certain foods, especially if you suspect you have a sensitivity or intolerance. Also notice how your body responds to medication or supplements designed to improve gut health.

- Consider incorporating supplements, foods, and beverages—like prebiotics and probiotics—that discourage unhealthy bacteria and infections in the gut. Do your own research and then ask your doctor before changing your diet or trying any new supplement or medication.

Talk to your healthcare providers or well-informed loved ones about ways they recommend caring for the gut.

Create Space to Feel Your Feelings

Making open space in your life and your schedule is one of the most powerful mindfulness and balancing tools to reach for in your self-care toolbox. It's easy for your life to become very busy and cluttered—sometimes this is circumstantial, other times it's habitual, and it can also be a way to avoid your feelings. Allowing open space in your schedule is a generous gift to bestow on that empath part of yourself. When you're perceiving more, there's simply more to process. Open space also allows you to ground back in to your own energy to touch base with your emotions—a big part of your natural GPS system.

This exercise will help you identify any blocks you have to creating more open space in your life:

1. Ask yourself: "What's the busywork occupying my time?" Busywork is work that keeps you occupied but doesn't have significant value. Use your intuition to arrive at the answer. Did you suddenly get an *image* of yourself at the office filing paperwork or archiving digital files that no one will ever need and that no one even asked you to keep? Maybe you immediately *thought* of how often you're the person picking up after the kids, realizing you need more support from your partner or even the children. Did you *hear* the word *cleaning* in your mind, knowing that you sometimes clean a little obsessively to the point of overkill? Perhaps you suddenly got the *feeling* that your beauty routine, like the way you prepare your hair every morning, has become way more time and trouble than it's worth. Look for ways to prioritize and streamline.

2. Ask yourself if there's anything in your life you're avoiding feeling. Sometimes when you have challenging, inconvenient, or confusing emotions, you can throw yourself into busywork or caring for others to avoid facing or exploring those feelings.

3. Ask yourself if there are people in your life you might enlist for help, opening up more space in your schedule. This could be a coworker, assistant, housekeeper, childcare provider, anyone you live with, or someone in your neighborhood.

4. Ask yourself if you're struggling with control issues. Are there things you're afraid to let go of because you believe only you can handle them? Analyze each responsibility, and objectively ask yourself if that's true or not. In some cases, it might be true—but in other cases it's probably not true.

If this exercise brought up a lot of feelings for you, talk to a counselor or trusted friend to work through these issues and create more open space in your life. The amount of space you can create might look different at different times in your life as circumstances shift—and that's okay. Your goal is simply to make creating open space a consistent part of your empath self-care routine.

Wrap Yourself in an Energy Blanket

An energy blanket is the ideal empath accessory, whether the weather outside is warm or cold. The following meditation is one you can do in the morning before you get dressed or leave the house, or anytime you want to prepare your energy to go out and meet the world in a balanced way—like before a big work meeting.

1. Sit in a comfortable position in a quiet spot and close your eyes. Feel the energy around certain parts of your body, like your hands and feet, starting to come alive. You might feel gentle pressure around those areas. Your energy body is saying hello!

2. Visualize a blanket being woven around you. Observe the textures of the wool or the brilliant sparkle of the thread. Your energy blanket might look like a favorite blanket you own.

3. Once your blanket has been magically woven, visualize it wrapping you up loosely. Picture it draping over your shoulders and covering your physical body but not in a tight or restrictive way. Notice how your comfortable blanket is big and generous, yet weighs nothing.

4. Feel your blanket on your skin—soft and soothing. Do you notice any other physical sensations like temperature changes, tingling, or chills? Notice how your blanket feels to your energy body. Do you feel a gentle energy pressure or forcefield around you?

5. Sit for a few minutes wrapped up in this snuggly, safe, and relaxing energy blanket. When you're ready, slowly come out of the meditation—but keep your energy blanket on.

As you go about your day, remember your energy blanket is still wrapped around you—real yet invisible. Your inner experience is everything!

QUIZ: Are You Giving Back and Being of Service?

Though it might seem incongruous, part of caring for yourself involves caring for others and being of larger service to the world. It is like a gift you give away, but when it's done in a balanced way, *you* receive bountiful benefits—in the amazing connection you feel to the world. It's been the great privilege of my life to work with clients one-on-one. The heartfelt thank-yous I receive from them surpass any other emotional experience I've had. Compassionate empaths feel more in harmony with life, and happier, when they are aligned with their purpose. Being aligned with your purpose isn't necessarily about your job title or your duties, but the purpose *behind* what you bring to others in anything you do.

Answer the prompts with *almost always, sometimes,* or *rarely:*

_____ I know what my soul gifts are, or what, in a general sense, I'm uniquely designed to contribute to the world.

_____ I feel like I live my purpose each day, and most days I'm excited or content about what I'm doing in the world.

_____ I can state my purpose in simple terms, like *teach, guide, provide, caretake, oversee, heal, nurture, assist, enhance, beautify, communicate, interpret, protect, analyze, build, create, innovate,* and *lead.*

_____ Whatever job I'm in, or whatever role I'm playing, it's often in the back of my mind to be a positive influence in the world.

_____ There are things I do on a regular basis—like donating, volunteering, or advocating—and lifestyle choices I make to help people, animals, or the planet.

_____ I'm passionate about making the world a better place, and there are practical ways I do my part.

_____ The way I show up in the world for others makes me feel deep joy, peace, or gratitude.

_____ In my daily life—at work, with my family and friends, in the larger world—I feel very connected to my heart.

_____ When I give to others, I'm able to receive compliments, compensation, and thank-yous with gratitude, presence, and humility.

_____ I don't believe I'm more special or more important than anyone else. But I know I matter, I'm worthy, and I'm needed.

_____ When I'm thinking too much about what I'm getting out of something, and losing touch with service, I feel off-balance.

_____ I've found a way to help others and get my own needs met financially and emotionally.

_____ I feel part of something greater than myself, connected to a larger humanity or connected to the living earth.

If most of these statements resonated as _almost always_ or _sometimes_ in your life right now, I'm so happy for you! If they didn't, don't judge yourself. You might have over-given and not taken enough care of yourself, and you might be in burnout. Or you might just be dealing with very challenging life circumstances and have a limited capacity to give right now. Concentrate on giving to yourself until your reserves are full enough to give more to others again. Sometimes we can simply lose touch with ideas like being of service and acting as a positive force in the world. If that's the case for you, devote yourself to interacting more harmoniously with the world so you can spread the good vibes and then feel them come back to you like a boomerang of love.

Align with Squirrel Energy for Financial Wellness

Squirrels? Yes! Those furry little creatures are masters at managing survival resources. Some empaths struggle with financial wellness because they can be too concerned with how their financial decisions affect others emotionally. For example, if an empath's spouse proposes quitting their job to follow their dream, the empath might want their spouse feeling happier—at any cost—so the emotional climate of the home is pleasant. The empath may put too much emphasis on people-pleasing and not enough on looking at the practical financial repercussions. Aligning with squirrel energy helps you be more strategic, and less emotional, about your financial resources. Finding this balance will help your mind, body, spirit, *and bank account*, stay more in harmony. Here are tips.

1. **Remember that abundance can be seasonal.** Squirrels know that in the fall there are lots of nuts, but winter brings slim pickings. Life is cyclical, so plan for financial fluctuations.

2. **Diversify!** Squirrels don't stockpile their resources in one spot— they store nuts in several spots! Speak to a financial planner about diversifying your resources or stream of income.

3. **Plan ahead, but enjoy today too.** Mimic the way squirrels meet their daily needs: eating some nuts immediately and stashing others. Squirrel energy isn't about hoarding, which can negatively affect financial flow in an energetic sense. Enjoy each day.

4. **Practice healthy selfishness with healthy habits.** Squirrels are in the habit of preparing for the future, and you can do the same by setting up automatic savings plans and sticking to a budget.

Make the screensaver on your phone or computer an image of a cute squirrel for inspiration!

Journal for Signs and Synchronicities

The universe—or God, the Goddess, Source, Spirit, your guides, your higher self—is always sending you helpful guidance. Recognizing these synchronicities, and receiving even more signs from the universe, is simpler than you might guess. This mystical manifestation process looks like:

- *Asking* for signs and synchronicities.
- *Observing* life to see what shows up.
- *Acting* on the guidance you receive.

Psychologist, psychiatrist, and scholar Carl Jung defined *synchronicity* as "a meaningful coincidence." For example, you might be pondering hiring an accountant to help you file your complicated taxes this year and *ask* the universe for a sign. The next day at the office you ask a coworker to lunch, and he says, "Oh, I can't today—I have a meeting with my accountant. They're a lifesaver!" This might be what Jung described as a *meaningful* coincidence—guidance from the universe to pay attention to! After you *observe* this, you might *take action* by asking your coworker for his accountant's contact information. How does the magic of synchronicity work? Everyone and everything is connected. Synchronicities could show up as:

- Well-timed opportunities.
- Musical messages you encounter on the radio or in a store.
- Helpful people, information, or resources coming into your life.
- Numbers and number sequences appearing on receipts, addresses, or email time stamps.
- Animals and nature.
- The wise or resonating words of others, which can even include overheard conversations in line or on the street.

The following journal exercise will help you learn to ask for and recognize more guidance from the universe.

1. Get out your journal and write a few sentences thanking the universe (or Spirit or your guides, etc.) for something you're grateful for. It could be as basic as shelter, or it might be celebrating a recent big win. Feel the gratitude permeate your energy—an authentically grateful energy is an ideal place to manifest from!

2. Now ask the universe for what you need help with—this is an issue you're wanting some synchronicities about. Write a few sentences on this as well.

3. Close your journal and go about your days normally for the next week. Stay present in the moment as often as you can, observing your world for signs. How can you discern genuine guidance from wishful thinking? As an empath, you have a heightened ability to "feel" guidance. When a possible sign appears, in any form, notice if your energy shifts. Does time seem to slow down? Does the moment feel pregnant with meaning? Do you experience any energetic or even physical changes? Do you return to thoughts about this sign continually throughout the day? Pay special attention to repetitive signs.

4. Consider taking action. Always run any intuitive guidance you receive through your head, your heart, and your filters of common sense and past experiences in the world. Speak to loved ones and consult experts for help on deciding when and how to act.

Engaging more mindfully with synchronicity is a way to engage more with the larger world. Everything is meant to work in harmony together, and you—or something you say or do—will be a synchronicity for someone else!

Fill Up Your Own Cup

Empaths are often drawn to roles and professions that traditionally emphasize giving and caretaking—like parent, teacher, nurse, or counselor. Yet empaths can bring a giving, caretaking energy to *any* job or role. Because energy-sensitives can feel intimately the suffering of others, they can therefore be more aware of suffering and motivated to help. Empaths who love to give and take care of others are lucky enough to experience the deep joy and contentment this path brings. When giving and caretaking are done in a balanced way, the giver receives so much!

Yet empaths must always be mindful about symptoms of burnout, which can include resentment, emotional or physical exhaustion, and pessimism. One way to avoid or heal burnout is to fill up your own cup—giving back to and nurturing yourself. This might look like having brunch with a new friend, checking out that art exhibit you're excited about, or making time to go to the store and get healthy, delicious ingredients for your lunches.

This exercise helps you get clear on how full, or empty, your cup currently is.

1. Imagine there's a magical cup located in your heart chakra that represents all you have to give to others. Get a mental picture of this cup—is it a delicate china teacup? A sturdy ceramic mug with pretty colors and patterns? Maybe it's a humorous mug with a silly saying written on it, or a mug with an inspirational word, like *love*. Let your higher self employ clairvoyance—the intuitive pathway that lets you receive guidance as mental images—to give you a picture of your cup.

2. Check how full your cup is. Again, use your clairvoyance to peer inside. Is your cup full or three-fourths of the way full with an

enchanting, sparkly liquid energy? Or is there a lot of room, showing how much you've given away lately? Maybe there's barely any sparkly magic energy inside. If your cup is half full or almost empty, shift gears and start emphasizing giving back to yourself.

3. Keep a mental list or a list in your journal of activities that fill your cup. Mine would include walking in the wooded greenbelt by my house, having phone dates with close friends who live far away, taking my time preparing healthy and delicious dinners, hanging out in person with loved ones, listening to podcasts where I learn something new or am reminded of something important, watching or reading a great story, tidying up and beautifying my home, getting lost in a fun creative project, dressing up, and sending care packages to people I love. Your cup is unique, and the way you fill it will be too!

One way to refill your own cup is to keep a close eye on your commitments. When considering if you should say yes to something, you might ask the other person for time to think, go somewhere private, and quickly close your eyes to picture your cup and how much energy you have to offer.

Surf the Changing Energies of the Zodiac Cycle

Astrology is an incredibly complex and fascinating subject. Each human has a very dynamic and intricate birth chart, and the planets are always moving in and out of different astrological cycles. As the sun moves into different signs throughout the year, everyone—regardless of their own personal chart or birthday—is affected by this astrological energy. For an astrology scholar, the zodiac sign the sun is currently inhabiting is just one piece of an amazing heavenly puzzle. However, we all know how essential and influential the sun's energy is to life here on Earth. The following are ways for energy-sensitive empaths to ride its waves of light and live more harmoniously with the heavens throughout the year:

- **Aries** (March 21–April 19): Be bold! Take healthy risks and be action oriented during the spring fever weeks.

- **Taurus** (April 20–May 20): Enjoy sensual pleasures/comforts, and emphasize stability.

- **Gemini** (May 21–June 20): Get intellectually curious, express yourself, and avoid boredom.

- **Cancer** (June 21–July 22): Cozy up your home, nest, and journal about your feelings.

- **Leo** (July 23–August 22): Put yourself out there and shine! Be generous with others and start a creative project.

- **Virgo** (August 23–September 22): Book a session with a healer, clean up your diet, and organize the details of your life.

- **Libra** (September 23–October 22): Bond with friends and family, emphasize balance, and look at life from other people's perspectives.

- **Scorpio** (October 23–November 21): Fire up the romance and do some deep inner healing work.

- **Sagittarius** (November 22–December 21): Travel, study another culture, explore spirituality, and be philosophical.

- **Capricorn** (December 22–January 19): Get down to business and get stuff done! Make practical, steady progress on your goals.

- **Aquarius** (January 20–February 18): Donate to a worthy cause and define your activism.

- **Pisces** (February 19–March 20): Be extra compassionate with yourself and others. Honor your connection to everyone and everything.

Numerology and astrology can be complementary mystical studies. I'm writing this book in 2020, which is a universal year of 4—that's a number that relates to earthly stability, order, effort, and laying solid foundations for the future. I'm hoping this book helps you have more earthly stability via a solid foundation of empath self-care!

Welcome Mercury Retrograde's Review Process

I recently informed a group of friends that it was Mercury retrograde—one rolled her eyes and sighed; another asked, "When is it over?"; and one friend simply exclaimed, "Aw, damn!" and walked away! The conventional wisdom about Mercury retrograde is pretty depressing—expect delays and miscommunications and don't make major decisions. But what's really going on during this astrological cycle?

A few times a year the planet Mercury *appears* to be moving backward in the sky. From an astrological angle, this signals an invitation for us on Earth to slow down, or go back and review, reflect, and revise. Mercury retrograde lasts for a few weeks and also has important pre-retrograde and postretrograde phases.

Empath and spiritual teacher Robert Ohotto suggests we each determine our personal Mercury retrograde message (after all, this planet is named after a Roman god who was a *messenger*). This message often catches your blind side, enabling you to improve and bringing into the light something you needed to work on or look at but were possibly unaware of before this cycle began.

Here are some techniques to help clarify your Mercury retrograde message.

1. Observe what shows up in your life during this cycle. Has an event happened that caused you to have a big revelation about yourself, someone else, or the world, like an issue you need to work on or acknowledge?

2. Notice anything secret, or previously hidden, coming to light. Even when these revelations are positive or pleasing, they are often still shocking. Perhaps it's even a buried emotion in yourself surfacing.

3. Keep a journal of the big synchronicities you experience during this cycle, then go back and see if you discern a pattern.

4. Find out which zodiac sign is influencing each Mercury retrograde. Visit your favorite astrology site to learn which sign, or signs, is currently affecting Mercury retrograde. Watch for themes in your life that coincide with the distinct energy of that zodiac sign.

Instead of dreading this cycle, use these techniques to make the most of the next Mercury retrograde. Facing issues you weren't aware of or weren't acknowledging but need to prioritize helps you achieve more balance in your life.

Growth can be painful—having things you need to work on or look at come front and center is never easy. Yet empaths often enjoy doing reflective inner work, and a few times every year the heavens give you the ideal opportunity with Mercury retrograde.

Practice Mindful Heartache with the News Cycle

Sometimes energy-sensitive empaths can "feel" devastating events—or waves of grief and fear from people, plants, and animals involved—even when they are not paying attention to the news cycle. Resist the temptation to completely ignore the news, though. Keeping up with current events helps you catch good news, offer your support when possible, and practice something called *mindful heartache*. This is a special term I heard empath and Good Vibe Tribe School founder Tess Whitehurst use to describe a practice I believe in strongly. Mindful heartache, or allowing your empath heart to mindfully feel in to the pain and suffering in the larger world, can:

- Increase your sensitivity in a healthy way, as your sensitive system is holistic. Mindfully tuning in to suffering helps you tune in to the blessings of the larger world too.

- Hone your techniques for managing challenging times in your own life by helping you master the balancing act of engaging witnessing energy and opening up to feel in to issues in the larger world.

- Give you the chance to make a difference. When you're informed, you can volunteer, donate, or make preventative lifestyle and political choices. Sometimes we take action only when *moved emotionally*.

- Assist you in getting clear on your boundaries. There will be times when—because of your life circumstances or mental and emotional states—you'll pull back significantly from the news cycle. Find balance in your engagement with the news.

Where can you practice mindful heartache with the news cycle? Or is this a time to pull back from the news? What stories can trigger your past wounds and require you to have clear boundaries?

Try Positive-Energy Speaking

While words and thoughts are powerful, they do *not* create or control your reality—though they can positively *influence* it. Empaths feel the energetic power of words. When we address important issues with hope—like in Martin Luther King Jr.'s "I Have a Dream" speech—without downplaying reality, positive speaking changes the world.

Have you offered a heartfelt apology or thank-you to someone and the positive energy behind your words made all the difference? Or have you started speaking with hope around an issue and your words positively influenced your actions, the actions of others, or the energy drawn to you?

The following exercise helps you practice positive-energy speaking.

1. Pick a day when you're feeling emotionally balanced and your energy feels neutral to engage mindfully in positive speaking.

2. Think before you speak today, checking that your positive-speaking filter is on. Strive for authenticity. If someone asks how you're feeling, and you're frustrated, share that. Add hopeful words too.

3. At the end of the day, observe any changes in your energy, emotions, actions, or outlook. Did your positive language have any effects on others?

Energy-sensitive empaths can have the gift of positive-energy gab!

When you talk about others, balance honesty with positive-energy speaking. Let's be real—at times, you need to vent. But even in those moments, remember that everyone has a soul, and in some magical way we're all connected. Any positive energy you are able to send another with your words may not be heard by their physical ears or seen by their eyes, yet may be felt by their soul.

Engage with the Survivor Archetype for Resiliency

Everyone reading these words is a survivor in one way or another, but have you ever mindfully thought of yourself as such? In my own life, I've leaned on the survivor archetype (or model) many times—as a child when my parents divorced, in middle school when I was bullied, as a teenager when my mother died from an AIDS-related illness, as an eighteen-year-old when I found myself out in the world on my own getting an apartment and working full-time, as a young woman when I navigated a series of illnesses in my late twenties through my mid-thirties, as a support system for loved ones battling addictions, and as an entrepreneur when I experienced financial hardships. On many of those occasions, I acted out of instinct, subconsciously employing the survivor archetype. There is a survivor inside of you who can take over at a moment's notice when necessary. Yet when you don't work with this archetype mindfully and consciously, it can be quite self-sabotaging.

Many of my sensitive empath clients are actually very tough. They are not hard or cold—they are resilient. For energy-sensitives who can easily pick up on other people's energies and emotions—and even the collective energies of the larger world—developing a tough resiliency is a valuable self-care tool. Being both sensitive and tough might sound contradictory, but these two character traits, or soul traits, are actually a harmonious partnership, balancing each other and helping to support empaths. Anything that an empath survives can further deepen their compassion for others.

Tips for empaths mindfully working with the survivor archetype:

- Remember that the survivor archetype is a natural part of you— you're sensitive yet also tough.

- Anything you can journey through and come out the other side of will change you. Know there will be gifts waiting for you on the other side of whatever you're surviving.

- Even experiences that are harrowing involve unexpected blessings and opportunities for you to grow, heal, and help others in powerful ways.

- People who have survived extremely difficult circumstances are hugely inspiring, especially when you need to activate your own inner survivor. Find documentaries or news articles or books about these people. Look around at the ordinary people in your life and ask yourself what they have survived and how they did it.

- A healthy way to engage with the survivor archetype is to ask for help. Trying to handle things on your own is unnecessary and unproductive. As you work with the survivor archetype, remind yourself that you want to make the journey as kind to yourself as possible.

- Always practice radical self-love when life asks you to survive something challenging or traumatic.

Sit with a journal and think back to some of the difficult events you have survived. Let this exercise empower you! If emotions come up, let that happen too. Write down some of the biggest lessons you learned along the way (so you can work with this archetype in an even more balanced way in the future), or how these experiences enabled you to grow, change, heal, or help others.

Build More Self-Confidence

After working with thousands of empath clients from all over the world and all walks of life, I've noticed that some empaths don't have as much confidence as they should. Whether it's in their professional or personal lives, empaths can underestimate themselves or be very cautious when assessing their value in the world—despite being wise, warm, giving, hardworking, conscientious people. The empath talent of sensing the energies and emotions of others could quickly set you up to feel real humility as an individual.

An empath friend told me about a memory from childhood, riding in the back of his parents' station wagon, heading into Kansas City one evening. Having grown up in a rural area, he was awed by all the lights on the horizon. "I remember thinking how many people must live in that city—all with their own hopes, dreams, and fears— and it struck me that I was no more important than any of them." Humility is an admirable characteristic, but it shouldn't exist in place of self-confidence—rather, they can balance each other. Build your confidence by asking others for evidence! The following are questions you can ask trusted, caring loved ones and colleagues.

1. What are my greatest natural strengths?
2. What positive character traits or skills have you watched me develop and master over time?
3. Do you recall an occasion I did something really impressive?
4. In what ways do I stand out from the pack?
5. Why would someone be lucky to work with me or be in a relationship with me?

Explain to others that this is an exercise you read about somewhere, and that you'd love to answer these same questions about them too.

Avoid Overexposure to Violence in Entertainment

Overexposure to violence is the norm in our society, but watching violence can have an especially detrimental effect on empaths. Because empaths can easily put themselves in someone else's emotional shoes, watching fictional characters fight for their lives is incredibly emotionally overstimulating for some empaths. And since empaths pick up on more and take longer to process stimuli than other people might, the violent video game an empath played on their lunch break could still be playing out in mental images as they close their eyes at night to try and sleep.

The following are general tips for avoiding overexposure to violence in entertainment.

1. Look away *and* mute the sound during a violent scene. Often an audience is given a few seconds' warning before something violent happens in a show. You could also switch the channel for a few minutes, take a bathroom break, or get up and stretch.

2. Find video games and movie genres that hardly ever involve violence, which will give your sensitive system a break.

3. Be choosy and deliberate about how many violent shows you watch. I might watch a historical drama that depicts violence related to another time period, for instance (so it's not just gratuitous).

If you'd like to take a more drastic step, take a sabbatical for three weeks for balance, avoiding games, movies, and shows with violent plotlines. Notice if you feel calmer, sleep easier, or have fewer nightmares. Your sensitivity may increase in healthy ways, as overexposure to violence has a numbing effect.

Activate Your Palm Chakras

Anyone can connect with the incredible energy present in the palm chakras. Often when I'm speaking to a client on the phone, walking in the woods, or holding an oracle deck, my palms will begin to feel warm—even talking about or thinking of these chakras can have a physical effect.

Practice feeling how real and alive your energy body is by mindfully engaging your palm chakras.

1. Hold your hands, palms facing each other, about 4 to 6 inches apart.

2. Think of the energy centers in your palms, or picture them in your mind as having a visible color or shape. It could be anything—like picturing two beautiful flowers opening up where your palms are or imagining a golden light there.

3. Hold your hands in this position for 2 minutes, and notice any physical or energetic changes. The open space between your palms will fill with energy, which might feel like a gentle weight or pressure.

4. Try this exercise with an empath friend: Have them place their hand in the open space between yours and ask them to describe what they feel.

Energy healing has many modalities and schools of thought. If you're interested in learning more about energy work, be sure to find an experienced and knowledgeable mentor.

Avoid Enabling Narcissistic Tendencies in Others

Clinical narcissism, as defined by the Mayo Clinic, is "a mental condition in which people have an inflated sense of their own importance, a deep need for excessive attention and admiration, troubled relationships, and a lack of empathy for others." Yet any human could, at certain times in certain situations, display narcissistic tendencies or act selfishly in a toxic way. We can all probably pinpoint, in hindsight, instances and relationships when we took advantage of others or disregarded the needs or feelings of others. Thanks to their keen sense of others' energies, empaths might accidentally at times foster narcissistic tendencies in others.

When someone is displaying this narcissistic behavior, it might be because they are really hurting inside, whether they are aware of it or not. A sensitive empath might pick up on that hidden wound and want to help. Or an empath might feel that this person is vital to them, or be very enmeshed in a codependent way, and not want to rock the boat and risk the relationship. Enabling could look like knowing someone's behavior is selfish, insensitive, and harmful to others and themselves to a toxic degree, yet allowing that behavior to continue unchecked and unchallenged—or even encouraging it.

The following are some possible steps to take as an empath if someone in your life is going through a narcissistic phase.

1. Acknowledge it to yourself. Don't just try to laugh off this behavior, blame it on eccentricity or circumstances, downplay it, or bury your hurt feelings.

2. If possible, diplomatically and kindly let this person know—through words or actions—that they have been behaving inappropriately. Remember that they are probably hurting, but alerting them to their

toxic behavior is in their best interests. It might help to start off the conversation by showing genuine concern for them, like saying, "I'm worried about you. You're usually so kind and compassionate, and lately you've been acting differently." It can help to read articles online from informed sites like PsychologyToday.com about confronting loved ones or dealing with someone in the throes of narcissism.

3. If the behavior continues with no sign of improvement, the person is unwilling to get help, you don't feel comfortable confronting this person, or this person gaslights you, you might need to distance yourself. Sometimes you can have little power in these situations if, for example, your boss is going through a narcissistic phase and it's causing you emotional distress at work. You might consider looking around for a new position, speaking confidentially to someone in your HR department, or just laying low to see if the phase passes.

Protect yourself, but also try to find a balance by giving others the awareness and grace *you* would want to receive. I've had relationships in the past where people let me know I'd crossed boundaries with them and held me accountable, yet still gave me space to change and stay in relationship to them. Relationships and people can and do heal—other times it's best to move on. There's a lot of information out there about narcissistic behavior and empaths. Articles or books written by healthcare professionals and experts can help you navigate this dynamic and your role in it.

Identify the Magical and Challenging Aspects of Being an Empath

Learn the cardinal traits of empaths and how they manifest in sparkly and not-so-sparkly ways. Emphasizing the magical and managing the challenging aspects will allow life as an empath to flow more harmoniously.

EMPATH CARDINAL TRAIT:
Can adapt to new environments easily by sensing the culture, energy, and emotional needs around them.

- **Magical Aspect:** Can fit in quickly in new work environments or new families.

- **Challenging Aspect:** Can lose track of their own needs or preferences.

- **Coping Skill:** When joining a new group, check in with yourself daily to see if there's anything about this new culture that you don't want to adopt, or to discern how the new group might adapt to *you*.

EMPATH CARDINAL TRAIT:
Compassion for other people's emotional experience.

- **Magical Aspect:** Have the capacity to be very caring because of their ability to feel someone else's emotions intimately.

- **Challenging Aspect:** Might struggle to express their own emotional experience to others honestly, sensing it may be inconvenient or upsetting to others.

- **Coping Skill:** Practice sharing your emotional experience, which gets easier with repetition.

EMPATH CARDINAL TRAIT:

Being deeply moved by music—perhaps the most emotional art form.

- **Magical Aspect:** Can use music to quickly transform their energy or mood.

- **Challenging Aspect:** Music infused with themes of heartbreak or rage, or any intense energy, can overwhelm and frazzle an empath.

- **Coping Skill:** Listen to a wide range of musical genres, artists, themes, and energy signatures (intense, neutral, and mild).

These are just a few of the cardinal traits of empaths—identify more that you've experienced. List them, along with their magical and challenging aspects. What are your coping skills?

Set Intentions with Full- and New-Moon Energy

The new moon (when it appears dark in the night sky) and the full moon (when this heavenly orb is fully visible and glowing) are considered powerful energy portals. Energy-sensitive empaths may notice an energy shift in themselves and in the larger world around the moon phases. Empaths are uniquely aware of the lives of others, so it's a good idea to use the new and full moon as a time to sit mindfully with your own life twice a month. One way to do that is by developing intentions. An *intention* is a means of focusing your mind, heart, and energy upon a purpose or goal. You might have the intention to be more considerate to friends and family, or you could set the intention to publish a book. Getting clear with yourself on what you want is the first step to experiencing it, and also enlists the universe's assistance in your manifestation efforts.

There are endless ways to approach moon rituals. After you try this exercise, look around for other methods. As you conduct this ritual, you might use candles, crystals, gentle mood music, oracle or tarot cards, or any sacred objects from your altar. You'll also want a journal and something to write with. Performing rituals timed around the cycles of nature is a wonderful way to stay in harmony with nature. This can deepen your connection to the earth and your awareness of its energy, which will bring more balance to your own energy.

1. In the two days leading up to a new or full moon, start asking yourself what your top three intentions are right now.

2. On the evening of the new or full moon, find a safe place to step outside and look into the sky for a few minutes. If the moon is dark, notice its absence. If the moon is full, bask in its brilliance.

3. If you have a private backyard or balcony and the weather is comfortable, you might stay outside for the ritual. Wherever you are, sit somewhere comfortable with anything nearby that helps you create a sacred vibe.

4. Sit still and take some deep breaths, letting your mind go blank. Anchor into yourself and the moment for 60 seconds or as long as it takes to feel centered. If there are certain spirit guides, angels, or ascended masters—like Mary and Buddha—you like to work with, acknowledge or call them in now in your thoughts or aloud. Remember that the energy of the moon will be harnessed and helpful too, so acknowledge it as well.

5. Now take out your journal and write down your three top intentions, with a few sentences about each. You might note any healthy sacrifice you are willing to make to harness more positive energy—like using less plastic to help the environment or not participating in negative gossip. Your sacrifice might have an end date, like sacrificing desserts for two weeks or joining in Dry January (abstaining from alcohol for the first month of the year). When you're done, close the journal and take three long, slow inhales and exhales. If you have a deck of divination cards, pull a single card for each intention and see what guidance shows up.

6. If you're outside or it's safe to step outside, close the ritual by looking again at the sky and thanking the moon for its clarifying, magnetic energetic assistance. If it's a new moon, remember that just because you cannot see the moon doesn't mean it's not there. If you can't get outside, look at pictures online of the full- or new-moon sky. Stay meditative as you blow out candles and put away crystals.

7. If you have time, flip back through your journal to the last intention you set with the new or full moon. (That might have been two weeks ago or it may have been several months ago.) Notice how your intentions have changed and evolved, and how some manifestations have shown up (perhaps in unexpected ways) or how others didn't—perhaps because of divine timing, other people's free will, outer circumstances, or your highest good being something different. If you like moon-phase rituals, you might keep a journal specifically for that purpose.

A variation on this ritual is to set your intention or plant a seed with yourself and the universe at the new moon, and then check in on its progress, course-correct, and ask for further intuitive guidance during your full-moon ritual.

Use Visualization to Manage Anticipatory Stress

For sensitive people, the days, weeks, or even months leading up to an event can be way more stressful than the event itself. To minimize anticipatory stress and balance your energy before an event that could potentially be overwhelming, try this creative visualization exercise. This technique may also help you stay more calm and present during the event itself. As empaths work to gently influence the energy of a future event in a positive way, it's possible this has a perceptible effect not only on themselves but also on others involved.

1. Identify an event that is causing you anticipatory stress, like a work meeting, a wedding, a tough talk you need to have with a loved one, a public-speaking engagement, or a date with your crush.

2. Picture yourself there and the event going well, adding in lots of sensory detail. Feel how relaxed, happy, or confident you are in this mental image, like imagining family members hugging and laughing at a reunion. If you know the event could potentially be very stressful, like confronting someone who crossed your boundary, picture yourself speaking to them calmly and directly and imagine them listening with an open mind.

3. Return to this positive mental image whenever your mind worries unnecessarily about the event. For example: You've planned everything for your big pitch meeting on Monday, but your mind keeps obsessing on details you've already double-checked, so you switch gears and go to your creative visualization of the pitch going smoothly or feeling confident and relaxed no matter what happens.

While making practical preparations is always important before a big event—like moving to a new home—this exercise can help you stay in balance so you don't overprepare and create unnecessary stress.

Gain Wisdom about the Empath Journey from Other Empaths

Some of my favorite books, courses, and podcasts are authored by empaths. Yet you can also gain valuable wisdom, tools, emotional comfort, comradery, and resources from the empaths already in your life. The following is a list of questions you might ask a friend, family member, or colleague who identifies as an empath.

1. When did you first realize you were an empath?
2. Were you always sensitive, or did this part of you gradually develop and emerge over time?
3. Have you ever had a sensitivity growth spurt? Why do you think that happened?
4. What's your favorite part about being an empath?
5. What's the most challenging aspect for you?
6. Are there other empaths in your family?
7. What are your favorite healthy retreat-and-recover activities?
8. Who are your favorite empaths to follow in the public eye?
9. Which empath authors or teachers have you learned the most from?
10. What's the best piece of information or advice for empaths you've come across recently?
11. What's your best coping skill when you're overwhelmed by energies and emotions around you?
12. How has being an empath been valuable in your personal relationships or professional life?
13. How has learning about your sensitivity brought more meaning or purpose to your life?
14. How have you made your home more of an empath sanctuary?

CONCLUSION: PRACTICE, NOT PERFECTION

Thank you, from my empath heart to yours, for reading this book. Working on it has been a priceless gift and journey for me. As you use the activities here to enhance or build your own empath self-care practice, remember that there will be seasons in your life when self-care feels more like a priority, or you have more time and resources to devote to your self-care. Other seasons, you will have to emphasize quality over quantity. As I tried to stay balanced and take good care of myself while I worked hard on this book, I was reminded that self-care is a practice—it's never about perfection.

The other interesting thing about self-care is that it's always needed in your life, unlike a goal you achieve so you can move on to the next one. I think a myth among empaths is that your self-care practice has to be very complex, involved, and time-consuming. Most empaths are looking to decrease the overwhelm in their lives, so an overwhelming self-care practice just won't do.

Don't feel like you have to fold in every exercise or ritual in this book to your current self-care practice. If you have a paper copy, you can hold this book between your hands, feel your heart and palm chakras activating, and then open the book to a "random" page. You might find that the exercise on that particular page isn't random at all but a synchronicity—an exercise that could be very useful in your life right now.

Thank you again for giving me another opportunity to do two of the things I love most—write and connect with other empaths. I'm sending you all my love and wishing you many blessings. Stay connected with me via social media, sign up for my free newsletter, or find out about my other books, workshops, and private intuitive readings at TanyaBlessings.com.

RECOMMENDED READING

Angel Intuition: A Psychic's Guide to the Language of Angels by Tanya Carroll Richardson

The Art of Extreme Self-Care: 12 Practical and Inspiring Ways to Love Yourself More by Cheryl Richardson

The Book of Sacred Baths: 52 Bathing Rituals to Revitalize Your Spirit by Paulette Kouffman Sherman, PsyD

Chakra Healing: A Beginner's Guide to Self-Healing Techniques That Balance the Chakras by Margarita Alcantara

The Empath's Survival Guide: Life Strategies for Sensitive People by Judith Orloff, MD

The Good Energy Book: Creating Harmony and Balance for Yourself and Your Home by Tess Whitehurst

The Highly Sensitive Person: How to Thrive When the World Overwhelms You by Elaine N. Aron, PhD

Sacred Space: Clearing and Enhancing the Energy of Your Home by Denise Linn

The Spirit Almanac: A Modern Guide to Ancient Self-Care by Emma Loewe and Lindsay Kellner

INDEX